OAK PARK

THE EVOLUTION OF A VILLAGE

DAVID M. SOKOL

Charleston   London

THE
History
PRESS

Published by The History Press
Charleston, SC 29403
www.historypress.net

Cover images: High school graduating class of the 1880s. *Courtesy HSOPRF*; Unity Temple. *Courtesy Lisa Kelly and UTRF*; Lake Street looking west. *Courtesy Downtown Oak Park*; Oak Park Library. *Courtesy Alan Becker.*

First published 2011
Manufactured in the United States
ISBN 978.1.60949.070.6
The author thanks Community Bank of Oak Park River Forest for financial support.

Sokol, David M.
Oak Park : the evolution of a village / David M. Sokol.
p. cm.
Includes bibliographical references and index.
ISBN 978-1-60949-070-6
1. Oak Park (Ill.)--History. 2. Oak Park (Ill.)--Social life and customs. 3. Oak Park (Ill.)--Economic conditions. I. Title.
F549.O13S68 2011
977.3'1--dc22
2011007654

CONTENTS

LIST OF ILLUSTRATIONS

ACKNOWLEDGEMENTS

Special thanks are due to the Community Bank of Oak Park River Forest for its support of this project by providing a generous donation toward the cost of acquiring many of the illustrations in the book.

The author of any local history is indebted to those people who were of direct help in providing illustrations, giving access to sources, sharing memories and reading drafts of the manuscript. This author is no exception to the rule but has the added responsibility of acknowledging, even indirectly, the many people my wife, Sandra, and I have worked with on the boards and commissions on which we have served. In addition, I would like to acknowledge the help I have received from others, as well as the people who shared their ideas with me and enriched the experiences I have had as I participated on panels and in study groups and while working on my prior publications.

For this book, I am particularly indebted to the following individuals, who either provided me with illustrations or directed me to other sources of pictorial material: Alan Becker, Oak Park Photography Club; Robert Biegler, Carleton of Oak Park; Jim Budrick, Sue Kornatowski, Joe Kreml and David Powers, Village of Oak Park; Jennifer Butler, Fenwick High School; Mark Finger, Oak Park Arts District; Frank Frigo, Community Bank of Oak Park and River Forest; Don Giannetti, St. Edmund Parish; Sharon Grimm and Deborah Preiser, Oak Park Public Library; Reverend Edgar Hiestand; Faith Humphrey-Hill, Oak Park Art League; Mitzi Irons, Oak Park Township; Lisa Kelly and Emily Roth, Unity Temple Restoration Foundation; Mary Liming, Oak Park Festival Theater; Frank Lipo, Historical Society of Oak Park and River Forest; Ellen Prus, Hephzibah Children's Association;

Roberta Raymond; Allison Sansone, Ernest Hemingway Foundation of Oak Park; Edward Solan, Oak Park Housing Authority; Diane Stanke, Park District of Oak Park; and Shanon Williams, Downtown Oak Park.

At the Village of Oak Park offices, Jan Jankowski in the office of the village clerk and Doug Kaare, the preservation planner, provided me with important information about village events, dates and the historic districts; at the Oak Park Public Library, Leigh Gavin gave me access to old records; Nancy Norton, longtime member of the board of the Park District of Oak Park, gave me access to the records she had culled from the history of that taxing body; Chris Jasculca of District 97 led me to chronological material and let me examine photographs; Sherlynn Reid shared information about the early Oak Park Exchange Congresses; Pat Koko gave me valuable information about the Community of Congregations; and Galen Gockel supplied background on the siting of village hall. At the Historical Society of Oak Park and River Forest, Tyler Watkins dragged out endless files and made photocopies for me. Frank Lipo, the executive director of the society, spent countless hours with me, pulling folders, dragging out heavy volumes of *Oak Leaves*, answering my questions, suggesting images to illustrate my points and striving to push me toward writing the best book possible. His knowledge is even greater than his efforts on my behalf, and were he not so busy helping other people with their work and research, he could well have been the author of this book.

Ben Gibson, the editor who commissioned this volume, has been ever ready to answer my innumerable questions promptly and helpfully. There were so many Oak Parkers who answered one of my many questions about their organizations, their own involvement in the community, their recollection of dates and the circumstances around specific events that I can not list them all here, but I thank them very much.

My wife, Sandra Sokol, not only brought to this project the knowledge she gained in her eight years in the Community Relations Department and sixteen years as the elected village clerk of Oak Park, but she also capped off a year of my absorption with the project by reading the manuscript. She brought both her clear eye and broad knowledge to correcting some of my more egregious errors. William Marshall—longtime professional editor, fellow village trustee (1977–81), dedicated member of the board of directors of the Oak Park Residence Corporation and dear friend—generously reviewed and carefully edited the draft manuscript. The final product, with its shortcomings, is my own responsibility.

INTRODUCTION

O ak Park has a reputation for clean government, with elected officials who can be reached at home and who see their service as ways of giving back to the community rather than as a source of patronage jobs or personal enrichment. Few stay in office very long; they usually opt not to stand for reelection. Given that reality, they tend to feel that if they only explained matters more clearly, their constituents would understand their positions, and it is often hard for the policymakers to understand the passions of those who don't agree with their decisions.

Here's a true story: a president of the village was talking with a citizen who was critical of a proposed mixed-use mid-rise development that would require financial assistance from the village. The president made some of the same points in different ways, trying to make the citizen understand why the development would ultimately be good for the community. Finally, the citizen said, "I do understand you, but I don't agree with you!"

Like many other suburban communities in the United States, the village of Oak Park has always had a deep and complicated relationship with the major city with which it shares a border. Like others, the village has had varied, and sometimes strained, relations with other neighboring communities. Those relationships have had the proverbial ups and downs, with moments of both cooperation and incidents of profound disagreement. The largest early disagreement resulted in Oak Park's disconnection from Cicero Township; the most recent agreement led to the decision to support Chicago before the U.S. Supreme Court regarding gun control. Whether the issues have been access to natural resources, matters relating to taxation or others, Oak Park has always tried to maximize its potential while remaining free of external control.

A defining characteristic of Oak Park has been the fact that all but one of its many taxing districts—village, township, park, library and elementary school—have had the unusual (for Illinois) advantage of having borders that are completely coterminous (*all* of Oak Park and *only* Oak Park). Only the high school district is shared with our much smaller neighbor, River Forest. Unlike so many communities in Illinois—a state with a very large number of taxing districts—the rarity of our coterminous districts has created opportunities for both cooperation and cohesion within the boundaries, though they have seldom reached their full potential.

Many communities in the United States have attracted attention because of natural sites of beauty, historic importance or architectural splendor. Though a handsome village, with stately trees and often large and handsome lawns, Oak Park has neither major waterways nor dramatic vistas. But it is rich in figures of historical importance, such as Ernest Hemingway, Doris Humphrey, Edgar Rice Burroughs, Percy Julian, Ray Kroc and William Barton. It is also blessed with the world's largest concentration of Prairie School buildings designed by Frank Lloyd Wright and his followers. The village's people, architecture and approaches to challenges have enhanced the reputation of the community and generated substantial and growing heritage tourism in recent times.

Finally, as a living and often self-conscious laboratory of the tension between progressive change and respect for tradition, Oak Park has found itself the subject of study and examination, in the press and in scholarly tomes, while the community also studies itself, reports its findings and maps its evolution as a village.

I am proud to call Oak Park my home.

Chapter 1

A PLACE BETWEEN THE LAKE AND THE RIVER

The sign on Chicago Avenue that identifies a Continental Divide is a reminder of the ancient geological reality of what was to become the village of Oak Park. The physical area of the future community was part of the large inland body of water that succeeded the Wisconsin Glacier. That sheet of ice began to shrink some fifteen thousand years ago, leaving a large body of water that was known to later scientists as Lake Chicago. The water covered the area that is now Chicago and its western and northern suburbs, but with the continued warming of the earth, the water receded and much of the geography of the area was formed. The divide in our area is the westernmost outcropping of what is known as the Niagara Shield.

This Continental Divide marked the place where, on the west side of the divide, the water flowed to the Des Plaines River, down to the Illinois River and to the Mississippi and, eventually, to the Gulf of Mexico. On the east, before the reversal of the Chicago River, the water would flow to the Chicago River, into Lake Michigan through the Great Lakes to the Niagara Falls, into Lake Ontario, then to the St. Lawrence in Canada and finally into the north Atlantic.[1]

In addition to what is now Lake Michigan, a substantial bay formed to the west of what is now Oak Park, and the hardwood forests of such woods as oak and hickory replaced the soft woods that covered the tundra. For hundreds of years, much of the area was a swamp, and the ice that still occupied the area to the north pushed seasonal rising waters over the high spit of land and into the river that French trappers and explorers first called the Eau

This sign on Chicago Avenue is one of the indicators in Oak Park that marks the Continental Divide that runs through the village. With the reversal of the Chicago River, all waters now run to the Gulf of Mexico. *Courtesy of the author.*

Plein—the name was given to the sap-filled trees along the river. The portage that they crossed in dry weather was called Portage des Chênes, after the many large oak trees in the area, and is the spit of land that later became known as Oak Park. Later, the French explorers changed the name of this branch of the Illinois River to the Des Plaines River.

Various Native American tribes hunted the area, and their portage routes and other trails became the roads of the future. Among the groups who hunted, fished and buried their dead in the area were the Fox, Potawatomi, Winnebago and Miami, but it is difficult to be certain which were in control of the immediate area at any given time. Artifacts found in the area point to meeting places, such as temporary and perhaps not-so-temporary settlements, but all of those were closer to the river and west of what became Oak Park. It is also clear that the divide stretched from the northeast area to the southwest, with its highest point in Oak Park being the area to the north of the present-day Taylor Park. Except at the highest point (and especially after heavy rains), the lower area from about what is now Harlem Avenue on the west to Kedzie Avenue on the east was referred to as Mud Lake.

French, Spanish and English, as well as other Europeans, had designs on North America, but the French trappers, traders, explorers and the clergy who accompanied them quickly took control of the area, sometimes intermarrying with native peoples.[2] As the pace of the fur trade slowed and the French concentrated their attention in other areas, Native Americans dominated the traffic along the portages in the area, with the Miami active and settled in the area that was to become Chicago. Indian warfare, particularly between the Fox and their various enemies, made for dangerous travel, and the portage to the Des Plaines and beyond became the fiefdom of whichever group had the upper hand at any given moment.

Throughout the eighteenth century, various claims were made for title to the area, though there was little traffic and no settlement there by Europeans. In September 1717, most of the Illinois area became part of the French province of Louisiana. However, no real surveys had been taken, and the boundary lines made it hard to know whether the portage area was included in Louisiana or remained part of New France. A French map of the area, drawn in 1718, refers to Lake Michigan and to the Des Plaines River as the Chicagou River.[3] Yet people other than the French had designs on the whole area around the lake, and in November 1738, the Virginia Colony's legislature created the new county of Augusta, including all of the Illinois territory.

With the start of the French and Indian War in 1754, the end of French control of the area was a forgone conclusion; Detroit fell to the British in 1759, and the area that included all of the Great Lakes territory was officially ceded with the Treaty of Paris on February 10, 1763. The whole of Canada and the area east of the Mississippi other than New Orleans came under British rule, but many French settlers remained, and a strong French influence would last until well into the next century. For the most part, Native American sympathies were with the French, who were more accepting of their way of life.

After the Declaration of Independence, and while both the British and the colonials were jockeying for position, almost no settlers were in the area from Lake Michigan to the far western part of the territory. To solidify its earlier claim, on December 9, 1778, Virginia claimed a swath of western land from its border to the Mississippi River, defining the western part as the county of Illinois.[4] With the signing of the Treaty of Paris on September 3, 1783, the British claims on the Illinois area were ended; the following year, Virginia traded its claim on the area to the federal government in partial settlement of the colony's debts during the Revolutionary War, and Connecticut surrendered its claim to any western lands, including Illinois, in 1786.

On July 13, 1787, Congress unanimously passed the legislation establishing the Northwest Territory, including all of present-day Illinois, and General Arthur St. Clair was appointed as the first governor. Two years later, he organized Knox County to include all of the area around Peoria and Chicago and its hinterland. Over the next decade, the area became part of several different counties, always with boundary lines so imprecise that it is hard to determine whether the Oak Park area was within them. As the Native American population was both small and transitory, nobody paid that much attention to this locale. With the Treaty of St. Louis in August 1816, the Fox and Sauk nations ceded a wide swath of land to the United States, including the longtime portage route between Lake Michigan and the Des Plaines River, and no further claims were made on the area. In 1818, Illinois became the twenty-first state.

During the next dozen years, the Potawatomi was the primary Native American group in the area, and the portage was in frequent use between Chicago and the area west of the Mississippi. Explorers with various government expeditions reported on the fertile ground and great prospects for farming in this area of Illinois, but a fear of continued Indian unrest and the lack of a solid settlement base limited permanent settlement. Political changes were frequent, with the area becoming, successively, part of St. Clair, Madison, Edwards and Crawford Counties before statehood and then Clark, Fulton and Putnam Counties, though Putnam was administered by Peoria County's elected and appointed officials. On January 15, 1831, the Illinois legislature established Cook County, incorporating all of present Cook and much of what are now Lake, DuPage, McHenry and Will Counties, with Chicago as the county seat.[5]

Chapter 2

EARLY SETTLEMENT

L ingering hostilities between the Native Americans and settlers through the emerging policies of removal were less present in the Chicago area than elsewhere after the Fort Dearborn Massacre of 1812. However, a brief Winnebago uprising in Wisconsin in 1827 and Chief Black Hawk of the Sauk's 1832 attempt to retake Illinois and Wisconsin must have been a deterrent on the potential for permanent settlement, other than in the emerging Chicago area, until early in the 1830s. With the signing of the treaty on September 26, 1833, between the United States and the United Bands (Chippewa, Ottawa and Potawatomi), the Native Americans ceded the remaining 5 million acres or so of land in Illinois in exchange for $500,000 and an equal amount to be paid as annuities over the coming years. The tribes agreed to move to reservations west of the Mississippi by the end of 1835.

The first attempt at an ongoing presence in the general area of the old portage route was the erection of a steam sawmill on the east bank of the Des Plaines River, just north of the old Lake Street trail, in 1831–32. The partners in this venture were Yorkshire men George Bickerdyke, a carpenter, and Mark Noble Jr., a butcher and land speculator, who had come to Chicago a year earlier. Though both maintained a primary identification with the heart of Chicago itself, their mill was to have a substantial impact on the settlement of both Oak Park and River Forest. Bickerdyke had purchased eighty acres of land along the river and, in addition to building the sawmill and selling the logs for construction of both cabins and streets in Chicago, made land available to the millworkers. Soon he was selling property to prospective settlers. Many of those workers were settlers of Oak Ridge, the early name for Oak Park.[6] There were also several other trails heading both east and west and north and south.

Bickerdyke was active not only in promoting his mill but also in encouraging immigration to the area. One of his old neighbors in Yorkshire was Joseph Kettlestrings, a carpenter who married Betty in 1828. With two small children, the family responded to the overly optimistic and romantic descriptions of Chicago that Bickerdyke had penned. They reached Chicago by way of Baltimore and Cincinnati in 1833, only to find muddy streets and unpainted cottages and shanties. As it was determined that he would be working at the sawmill, Kettlestrings moved on toward the Des Plaines River, pausing to place a claim to 173 acres on the richly wooded high ground on and west of the Continental Divide in what is present-day Scoville Park. But in order to get his young family housed and fed, he moved into a log cabin near the mill, where Joseph worked for two years before obtaining part ownership. He then moved onto his "claim" and built a home with logs from the mill. The house was located on the part of his land closest to his work, next to the western border of present-day Oak Park.

Kettlestrings soon enlarged the home, both to provide room for the family that eventually included eleven children and also for the business opportunity he saw in providing lodging and food for travelers to and from the west. The family first offered room and board, with Mrs. Kettlestrings doing the cooking and cleaning for the guests. However, he soon advertised the establishment as Oak Ridge Hotel in Kettlestrings Grove, and their existence was noted in Chicago. As the Kettlestringses—like Noble and others of the Englishmen who joined them—were strongly antiliquor Methodists, no alcohol was served at their hotel, and they were active later in the move to keep it out of Oak Ridge.

Kettlestrings astutely saw the potential for the area and the growth of population in Chicago and farther west of Oak Ridge, especially because of both the federal and the state government's commitment and funding for the proposed Illinois and Michigan Canal. He bought a "quarter section" of land that stretched from the present Oak Park Avenue to Harlem Avenue and from Chicago Avenue on the north to the present Lake Street El and Metra line. The cost of the land was $215.98, and the official deed of sale was signed by President Martin Van Buren on March 20, 1837. In later years, Kettlestrings purchased more than two hundred additional acres, both north and south of his original stake.[7]

As there were no schools anywhere near the home, the farm was rented out and the Kettlestringses moved to Chicago for close to a dozen years, returning in 1854. Soon, Kettlestrings began subdividing and selling his large parcels, with the first large piece sold to R.K. Swift in 1848, after which a modest number of settlers moved in. The area became officially the Kettlestrings subdivision in 1856.[8]

Abram Gale moved to Chicago from Massachusetts in 1835 and operated a meat market in Chicago, while his wife sold hats to Chicago's growing population of women. Like Kettlestrings and many others, the Gales bought a large parcel of land, at the 1837 sale in the higher and drier area, about eight miles west of Lake Michigan. The original 320 acres of what became Galewood cost about $200 and covered the area directly east of Oak Ridge and north of the area called Ridgeland. His son, Edwin, and others of the Gale family were to become major figures in Oak Park's history. Other early settlers were primarily of English stock, though there were also some German families. One was that of Albert Schneider, a cobbler who became

Albert Schneider Jr.'s part of his father's landholdings east of Harlem Avenue became the heart of a florist business with a greenhouse, several Oak Park stores and another store at a local cemetery. *Courtesy of Historical Society of Oak Park and River Forest* (hereafter *HSOPRF*).

a substantial landowner and farmer and whose descendants owned a major greenhouse and florist shops and also gave their name to a street in the area east of what is now Harlem Avenue.

That real settlement was here to stay was confirmed when the Galena and Chicago Union Railroad laid its tracks from Chicago along the same old portage route that had been the road of choice between the far western part of the state and Chicago since the time of the Native Americans and French trappers. The station opened during 1848–49 and was located just west of today's Harlem Avenue. At first the only scheduled trains were freight trains, though local lore says that one of the major figures in Oak Park history, James Scoville, rode the caboose into downtown Chicago in an hour at an early date. When the growing population soon called for access to the city from the area, regular passenger service was added to make it the first commuter line in the region. Chicago's first mayor, William B. Ogden, was one of the principal figures in developing the railroad, and he later got involved in real estate in the area.

In spite of rail transportation going from east to west, the old trails remained in use for decades. A street named Pennsylvania Avenue (later renamed Lake Street) was a toll road and had been graded in 1842. The five-cent toll that was paid at what is now Austin Boulevard was resented, causing locals to try to bypass it on the cow path that was to become Chicago Avenue, known as the "Big Ditch." Other hardy souls took the ungraded Madison Street. Decades later, one of Kettlestrings's grandchildren was to reference the 1860s, noting that "the route of the old lumber road through the forest in north Oak Park was plainly marked when I was a boy. We called it the 'Indian Trail'—perhaps it had been that originally."[9] James Scoville and H.W. Austin obtained the concession to run the toll road in 1869, and they maintained it and collected the tolls for a decade. As we will see, Scoville had his hand in many of the ventures and projects in the area. As president of Prairie State Bank in Chicago, he had a substantial income and access to funds for civic improvements and used his influence to affect land policy as well as community development.

The next twenty years saw a solid population growth, the subdivision of most of the early major land purchases and the arrival and settling in of several of the major families who began to shape the community and its institutions. J.W. Scoville, Milton Niles, Orrigen W. Herrick and Albert Schneider were among the pioneers, though Scoville and Niles were interested in land for investment and subdivision purposes and Schneider for farming and building a family business. Schneider and other early German

The Scoville mansion was the home of the early land speculator and developer of Oak Park who played such a major role in its formative years. James Scoville's mansion stood at the heart of the park that now bears his name. The home was demolished in 1912. *Courtesy of HSOPRF.*

settlers developed their properties just east of the present Harlem Avenue and north of Chicago Avenue, while the Scoville and Niles subdivision was south of the railroad. The latter two began to subdivide in 1863, releasing other parts of their property again in 1868 and the rest in stages in the 1870s. Most of the homes built there were on large lots, for the settlers' large families, and included a barn for the horses and buggy, while the scarcity of stores and markets made it wise to have a yard for growing vegetables and for keeping fowl and sometimes other livestock as well.

The area that was known as Ridgeland was named after the high ground near the Continental Divide. Scoville, Ogden, Joel Harvey, Josiah Lombard and, later, E.A. Cummings all bought property there, though Scoville concentrated his attention in the area between the present Oak Park and East Avenues. Many of the streets in that part of today's Oak Park were named after those early speculators and developers, with both a street and an entire community named after H.W. Austin, who moved there in 1858. Some of these men resold or subdivided their property as soon as there was a profit to be made, while others didn't do so until after the Civil War or even after the Great Chicago Fire.

The area prospered and soon had its own fire department and some other services, even before all of the area was fully subdivided. And while many of the settlers of the area were engaged in farming and local trading, others were

This early photo is of a home on the ridge of the Continental Divide, at North Avenue. Subsequent grading for construction purposes has lowered much of the land at the apex of the ridge. *Courtesy of HSOPRF.*

there for the spacious properties on which to build their homes and some to escape Chicago taxes. While only a few commuted at first, later more and more men were living in what is now Oak Park and working in Chicago.

Ridgeland and the then Oak Ridge enjoyed a friendly rivalry, with many of the major pioneer families and developers holding property in both communities. Each had basic services and some stores, with a general store at today's Harlem Avenue and Lake Street as the major "anchor" in 1856, the same year that the name "Oak Ridge" was changed to "Harlem." Many more stores opened with the rapid growth of the area after the Civil War. Then, returning veterans such as William Beye, E.A. Cummings, Anson Hemingway and Orin Peake joined the earliest settlers in opening stores and setting up their professional practices in Oak Ridge. The businesses that slowly moved east from Harlem Avenue were usually on the first floor of two-story buildings made of wood, often with the merchant or professional living upstairs with his family. In 1867, bowing to public pressure, the name "Oak Ridge" was reapplied to the western community.

The earliest post office in the area had been located at the Ten-Mile House at Lake Street, just west of the Des Plaines River and then the home of William Noyes, and much of the area was known as Noyesville before the township boundaries became fixed.[10] Few records exist for this period, but it is known that the post office for the whole area was organized on August 10, 1846. It moved several times, and had changes of name, before finally moving to what is now Oak Park in 1871 and taking the name of Oak Park Post Office. Based in O.W. Herrick's general store, the post office served all of Oak Ridge, Ridgeland and River Forest, as the latter didn't have its own facility until a decade later.

Both Oak Ridge and Ridgeland, as well as several of the surrounding communities, had been included in Cicero Township when it was formed in 1857, and the municipal offices were located in the Austin area of the original six square miles. In the first township election, the Oak Ridge/ Ridgeland contingent was well represented. Of the mere fourteen votes cast, Joseph Kettlestrings and James, William and George Scoville were all based in the area, and several immediately took leadership positions. William H. Scoville became supervisor; James A. Scoville, assessor; George Scoville and Joseph Kettlestrings, commissioners of highways; George Scoville, justice of the peace; and Joseph Kettlestrings, overseer of the poor.[11] This level of involvement by the future Oak Park leaders was not only due to the paucity of eligible voters but also reflected the hopes and plans that those men had for their community.

This little building served as the first school, as the temporary home of many congregations and as the headquarters of the temperance movement in Oak Park, as well as for many community functions. It was finally razed in 1901. *Courtesy of HSOPRF.*

At the time of the election, both the Oak Ridge and Ridgeland communities (hereafter referred to as Oak Park) had recently begun to attempt to respond to the need for education in order to create a viable living environment for local families. Joseph Kettlestrings had permanently returned to residence in 1854 and, as he had only moved to Chicago in order to educate his children, decided to loan a piece of property at what is now Lake Street and Forest Avenue as a school site, with the stipulation that it would be returned to him when a permanent school was built.

A one-story frame building was erected the following year, serving both as the local school and as a meetinghouse for the community and its religious organizations. A principal was hired, and the school was started with fewer than twenty pupils. A somewhat haphazard organization with a changing cast of administrators was the rule for the first several years until external forces made a real school a possibility. With the creation of the township of Cicero in 1857 came the structure of a school township as well, and School District No. 1 became the boundaries of the present-day elementary district, the township and, later, the village of Oak Park. All 230 lots that were offered were sold that year, and the proceeds were used for the support of a school fund.[12] After a few years in the temporary Kettlestrings building, a lot was purchased, and the first public building, Central (later Lowell) School, was created in 1859 at a cost of about $20,000. Joseph Kettlestrings and James W. Scoville were two of the three members of the first board of directors, with the former serving continuously until 1877. A board of education replaced the board of directors in 1887.

Churches and other religious organizations were established at an early date, with the pioneer Methodists having services in the area that encompassed Oak Park and the communities of Thatcher and Austin soon after Kettlestrings arrived. A traveling Methodist preacher started the Union Ecclesiastical Society in 1856. Within a few years, there were several congregations, with a nondenominational group (1863), as well as Baptist (1873), German Evangelical (later Lutheran in 1864) and Presbyterian (1860–61) churches. A group of Unitarians and Universalists who attended the nondenominational Oak Ridge Church left the congregation when it decided to affiliate with the Congregational Church and formed Unity Church (1871).

Early congregations met in homes, rented facilities and, after 1855, at the small building on Kettlestrings's property that was the first school. Until the population exploded following the Great Chicago Fire, services were led either by laymen or itinerant ministers. But other faiths had their place in early Oak Park as well, even when there were very few local members of those religions and they had to journey out of the immediate area to worship with others. Episcopalians met in River Forest until 1879, the Roman Catholic Church had a mission in the area beginning in 1865 and a parish that straddled Austin and Oak Park in 1889, decades before a building was erected. One of the early business owners was Jewish, though it is not known if there were others—or if or how he worshiped.[13] Though not everyone was welcomed with open arms, either at this early date or through the years, this mixture of religions is an indication that the community had an unusual level of diversity at an early date.

With a secure township government in place, growing places of worship and the start of a real school for families, the original purchasers of much of Oak Park's land began to subdivide in earnest. The population began to grow, with a combination of farmers, local business and professional men, as well as the families whose heads commuted to work in Chicago. In 1863, James Scoville and his partner, Milton Niles, subdivided their holdings south of the railroad that traversed Oak Park and built several houses there in the next few years. Scoville subdivided his acreage between Lake Street and Chicago Avenue to the north and between Oak Park and East Avenues to the east in 1868. The original Chicago and Galena Railroad had been subsumed into the Chicago and Northwestern in 1864 and had greatly increased commuter service, enabling many more businessmen to live in Oak Park while working in Chicago. All of these factors helped the men who had purchased the large tracts of land market their properties when they subdivided while also making them wealthy supporters of the community. At the same time, their experiences, beliefs and social agendas made them solid Oak Parkers who nevertheless valued their proximity to and activities in Chicago. As a local booster was to succinctly say when expressing that relationship: "In no self-righteous or unsympathetic spirit does Oak Park hold herself aloof: she rejoices in the great things of Chicago, and cherishes her own ideals."[14]

Chapter 3

EXPANSION AFTER THE CHICAGO FIRE

The population of both Oak Ridge and Ridgeland had been growing slowly but steadily through the 1860s, and the existence of both a local post office and school helped unite the two communities. In addition, several of the major landholders had properties in both areas of the township and were a significant force in support of increased and shared services. There were probably about five hundred people in the area at the start of the 1870s, when the highly damaging Chicago fire occurred on October 8, 1871. With close to four square miles of the downtown eradicated in the two days that the conflagration raged, the direct impact was felt not only throughout the city itself but also in the suburbs, where the men who worked in offices or owned stores in Chicago lived.

Even before the fire was contained on the tenth, Oak Park residents knew that the effects would be profound. Merchants in Chicago who lived in Oak Park were wiped out, as the banks and insurance companies couldn't cope with the unheard-of scale of the loss. James B. Herrick, a grandson of Kettlestrings, described how "[a]s soon after the fire as it was deemed safe, Oak Park citizens, especially the housewives, collected sandwiches, crackers, hard-boiled eggs, milk, coffee, and other suitable foods to send to the sufferers." His grocer father and A. T. Hemingway (Ernest's grandfather) drove "through the still hot streets and to the sands of the lake shore on the North Side and distributed the food."[15]

Edwin O. Gale, who had his pharmacy business in the city, left a record of what happened: "While at the breakfast table that Monday morning,

A.T. Hemingway called and informed us of the great catastrophe which had engulfed the city."[16] Gale took the first available train to the city and rushed across the Chicago River, as the Wells Street Station had been destroyed. He found his partner, but his store and all of his recently ordered stock had been destroyed. Two of his Oak Park neighbors made important offers to him, showing the way they looked after each other and supporting the notion that generosity knew no ethnic or religious boundaries. Gale wrote how Joseph Kettlestrings "came to my house and asked me if I could use $5000," which he offered to lend Gale until he got on his feet, with no security but his promissory note. As Gale needed $10,000 to restart his business, the old settler loaned him that amount, with a mortgage on his home.[17] William Steiner owned the general store in Oak Park, and he offered Gale unlimited credit to stock what he needed to survive and support his family for a year, saying, "I have almost everything your family require [sic], dry goods, groceries, boots and shoes, hardware, crockery, clothing, and everything a general store contains…and when perfectly convenient you can pay me without interest."[18] Gale pointed out that Kettlestrings was a Methodist and Steiner a neighbor and a Jew but that both were selfless and helpful men in that time of distress. We can also assume that Gale was not the only local person helped by these men and other neighbors after the fire.

As everyone who lived in the path of the fire had to find new lodgings, many people who could afford it moved to Oak Park, the closest suburb that had the array of institutions noted as being in place. Land costs were rising quickly, and the property that could be purchased for $1.25 per acre at the initial sale in the mid-1830s sold for $1,000.00 an acre in 1871 and for $3,000.00 an acre by 1874 in the Oak Ridge area, while an acre could be had in Ridgeland for about $700.00.[19] The price differential reflected two major variables: the land east of the Continental Divide was lower and less well drained, and the stores and schools, all being closer to Harlem Avenue, made the western area more convenient for family life. But the Ridgeland area did grow as well, and its residents were soon agitating for both public services and economic development. And as the population swelled dramatically, more and more businesses opened in the area near Steiner's General Store at Harlem and Lake, establishing the current downtown Oak Park at an early date.

Within two years of the Chicago fire, a blacksmith, a contractor and a druggist had opened stores, along with the introduction of a hardware store and a second general store. A painting contractor, a bakery, a harness maker, other food stores and one of Edwin Gale's drugstores quickly joined those businesses. Professional offices often occupied the second story of the wooden two-story buildings. With business and the population booming, the railroad station was moved east of Harlem to the business center in 1872. Soon, as growth was so rapid and the demand was so great, the first three-story brick building was erected at Lake and Marion Streets in 1876. Given the lack of public buildings, the large rooms on the upper floors were often the site of lectures, concerts and even dances and social events. At that time, and until the early twentieth century, the streets were numbered, with the lowest numbers starting at Harlem and running east.

Henry W. Austin was a successful salesman who had purchased land from Kettlestrings and built his large home at Lake and Forest after his marriage in 1859. He later became a major real estate magnate in the period, purchasing 280 acres in the western part of Cicero Township and leading its development through subdividing and public works. But Oak Park remained his home for the rest of his very active life (in sales, in real estate, in banking and in politics). Austin was also a key figure in banking, opening the Oak Park State Bank in 1892 and in 1899 absorbing the Dunlap Brothers Bank that had preceded it. He was generous in keeping the small building on the

Palmer's hotel replaced Betty Kettlestrings's inn as the place to stay when visiting Oak Park or on the way westward. It may have housed the tavern that Henry Austin bought to rid the town of liquor. *Courtesy of HSOPRF.*

former Kettlestrings property available to both church and civic groups and was deeply committed to Oak Park, to his family and business and, along with Joseph Kettlestrings, to the temperance movement.

Austin renamed the little building Temperance Hall, which became the headquarters for the battle against alcohol in Oak Park. The tale often told of Austin's attempt to keep liquor out of the community bears repeating, as his success was to have strong, though mixed, repercussions for the community for a century. Austin was a member of the Illinois Twenty-seventh General Assembly from 1871 to 1872, representing the often changing boundaries of the area. Thus, he had some real clout and was apparently able to convince the Cicero Township leadership to issue no more liquor licenses in Oak Park. He then purchased all three of the saloons that held licenses and closed them down. The story is that the last owner held out for a very high price and that Austin finally met that price and proceeded to empty the stock into the street.

Austin followed that success by getting the state legislature, in which he served as an elected representative, to pass an early dram shop law that made local option possible.[20] No more liquor licenses were issued, and the area, later the village, was to remain dry for more than one hundred years, with major support by a large local chapter of the Woman's Christian Temperance Union and the majority of the men who controlled political life in the community. Years later, the famous local minister William Barton was to describe Oak Park as a dry community as two teamsters were bringing building materials from Chicago. One said to the other, "I've never been out there before. How shall I know when we get to Oak Park?" "When the saloons stop and the church steeples begin" was the answer.[21] The success of Austin and his allies in keeping liquor out of the community is an early example of how the civic elite were able to influence the shape of the community to their satisfaction, and it is probably safe to say that the German men and many of the travelers who stopped in Oak Park were not happy about their inability to have a beer or two.

The churches were certainly a major presence in the early years, and they remained an important influence within the community. Indeed, people who worshiped together tended to also unite in various organizations and on behalf of civic betterment projects. Though an unusual number of changes occurred in the late 1870s, it was only as a result of rapid population growth, new demands and enough commitment on the behalf of the citizenry. Education was a priority. The high school division of the school district had been started in 1873, and the first graduating class consisted of only three

This image shows just how rural and sparsely settled the area was around the time of incorporation, looking west into Oak Park from Austin Boulevard. *Courtesy of HSOPRF.*

pupils. A rented space had been secured for primary education in Ridgeland in 1874, but with the growth of the population, additional school facilities were needed in both Ridgeland and Oak Ridge. The first superintendent of schools was appointed in 1876, and he oversaw two expansions of the Central School and the erection of a new brick building, at first named Ridgeland School House, in 1879. The latter, a small brick building, was built at a cost of $8,000. But within a few years, additional space was needed in Ridgeland, and new buildings were required to serve north and south of the central population core, as population pushed into those areas.

It was James W. Scoville who led many of the civic improvement projects, even after giving up control of his Lake Street toll road and selling it to the township in 1878 for $325. In support of the community and to further the value of the lots he was selling through subdivision of his properties, he began to develop a plan for providing water for his home and properties.

Up through 1878, cisterns and wells had been the only way fresh water was available, often with shortages. Scoville started constructing a private reservoir on his properties that year, though it took five years to complete. At the same time, Ira Owen offered to supply fresh water to his neighbors on Maple Avenue and vicinity if they would pay the construction costs of pipes from his artesian well.[22] Other signs of growth included an increase in the number of trains provided by the Northwestern Railroad, with three morning and three evening trains in the schedule by 1878 and fifteen in each direction less than a decade later. In the early 1880s, Scoville and other private citizens agitated for a station at Oak Park Avenue and then paid for it themselves to ensure that it would be built.

Not surprisingly, Scoville was also a leading and guiding force in cultural affairs, as well as business matters. As a member of the Congregational church, he suggested that it establish a library for the use of members. It was familiarly known as the "Pastor's Library" when a library room was dedicated to that purpose in the new building in 1873.[23] The congregation voted to make an annual financial commitment to fund the library, but the Panic of 1873 caused its members to retrench, and the collection stalled at about fifty or sixty volumes.

In 1882, a Library Association was formed by a group of men who were all active in the community; they set up their membership organization in one of the wood-frame stores on Lake Street, and it was open to members three days a week. The membership fee was $5.00 for men and $2.50 for female members, to cover the cost of purchasing materials and pay the librarian $10.00 per month. "All of the ministers in town, as well as the teachers, were given complimentary memberships, as were all 'young ladies in the families of members.'"[24] The membership fee was inadequate to buy much, so a charge of $0.10 for a book and $0.05 for each magazine borrowed, each week, was instituted. The association moved to rooms in the Steiner Building at Lake and Marion and gradually built the collection to over 1,500 volumes.

In 1883, James Scoville publicly committed $75,000 toward the creation of an organization and building that would further the education of the citizenry, and the plans included a library and the display of art. Eventually, when that amount of money proved insufficient, his gift amounted to the value of the lot on which the library was built and more than $82,000 for the building itself.

A board of local men was incorporated, and a well-known architect, Normand Patton, who lived in Oak Park, was commissioned to design the building; it was dedicated in 1888 as a private subscription library, and a librarian was hired. The Library Association donated its books and disbanded, and the First Congregational Church donated its small collection as well. Within three months, enough people had subscribed that there were funds to order additional books. The following year, life memberships were initiated at fifty dollars, and the third floor of the building was outfitted as

The Scoville Institute, the home of Oak Park's first library and cultural center, was designed by Normand Patton in a Romanesque Revival style influenced by H.H. Richardson. *Courtesy of HSOPRF.*

a gymnasium, though that facility lasted for only a dozen years. Expensive to run, with the need for instructors and the cost of replacing equipment on a regular basis, the gym was also noisy and proved its incompatibility with the other aspects of the building. By the end of the decade, there was a substantial collection, and the facility was one of only a dozen American libraries to have a full set of the Congressional Record.

The Scoville Institute, as the building was known, became the major community center, replacing Temperance Hall and the upper rooms at the Steiner Building. The auditorium on the second floor was used extensively for lectures and musical events, while the parlors were utilized for meetings and smaller recitals through the rest of the century. Along with the desire for a solid educational system, and with the support of the subscription library, was the interest in broader cultural enrichment for the community. It has already been noted that lectures and recitals had been staged on the second floor of several buildings before the Scoville Institute was opened.

The University of Chicago offered a series called "Community Lectures" at the institute, and there was a forum and various other aspects of organized adult education in the 1890s. The visual arts were slow to take hold, though several artists were known to have lived and worked in the community in the 1880s and 1890s, and the Scoville Institute provided the first real opportunity for exhibitions. Theater was less of a draw, with some lingering feelings that actors were a dissolute lot, so it was only after the turn of the century that there were regularly scheduled and advertised theatrical performances.

Music seems to have been the major form of cultural expression in early Oak Park, with the community boasting a number of private music schools and several amateur music groups. The earliest seems to have been the Oak Park Orchestra, which was founded in 1880 and, under the directorship of William Corbett, lasted about four years. There were six members, including

John Farson's property contained much more than his impressive national landmark house designed by G.W. Maher in 1897. The grounds and outbuildings, and even the architect-designed fence, were part of the ambiance, down to the exotic gardens, stables and clock tower. *Courtesy of HSOPRF.*

H.W. Austin playing second violin. In 1886, the Oak Park Silver Cornet Band was founded with thirteen members, using rented space in the building on the northeast corner of Lake and Harlem. The Oak Park Choral Society was founded in 1897, with Grace Hall Hemingway as its first director. Music schools were vital for nurturing would-be musicians and amateurs and for developing an audience for professional concerts.

The Oak Park School of Music, founded in 1875, was housed on North Boulevard, near Oak Park Avenue. It promised high-quality instruction without the necessity of traveling to Chicago. Other schools were often branches of already established Chicago institutions. Many professional concerts were offered in the community for private societies and in members' homes, in churches and in more public venues. The Oberlin Glee Club visited in 1897, singing at the First Congregational Church; the Beloit Glee Club, Boston Ladies Symphony Orchestra and others performed locally. Later, John Farson opened the spacious grounds of his home for open-air concerts. He was also the president of the Rubinstein Club, which was organized in 1895 and presented both instrumental and vocal concerts to the public. Its music director was Mrs. P.S. Hulbert, one of many socially prominent women who provided leadership in cultural matters. The leading gentlemen's organization, the Oak Park Club, sponsored Summer Evening Band Concerts at its headquarters starting in 1894. Admission was free, but it cost ten cents to either rent a chair or to lock up one's bicycle. So much was offered by the turn of the century that it was probably not an exaggeration when a local paper noted that "[t]here is no place in Illinois where there are so many musical people to the square inch as there are in the pretty little suburb of Oak Park."[25]

The other major component of literacy is the availability of newspapers, yet it is hard to establish when the first newspaper was published in the Oak Ridge/Ridgeland area. The first documented attempt was the *Oak Park Record*, which appeared for only one issue in July 1874, announcing itself as "an occasional publication." It included wood engravings of churches, the homes of leading citizens and so on, as well as material on both Oak Park and River Forest written by different authors.[26] Other newspapers came and went for the next decade, with various Chicago- or Cicero Township–based papers often including news of and for Oak Park readers. Three attempts at providing a local paper were made in the early 1880s, including the more successful *Weekly Review*, but none was able to keep going. A successful publisher in Chicago grew his regional paper to include a regular Oak Park column in the Cicero section in September 1883. The editor, William Halley,

Above: The Oak Park Club, founded in 1890, later purchased this large home on the northwest corner of today's North Boulevard and Forest Avenue. When the clubhouse was destroyed by fire, the members built the large brick building that was its home until the club was disbanded in the late 1980s. *Courtesy of HSOPRF.*

Left: The *Oak Leaves* resulted as the merger of earlier local newspapers and has been a major newspaper of record since 1902. It continues today as one of the many periodicals published by Pioneer Press, now a division of the Sun-Times Media Group. *Courtesy of HSOPRF.*

made it a suburban paper in 1885 and renamed it the *Cicero Vindicator*. Later it became the *Oak Park Vindicator*, purchased the *Weekly Review* and put it out of business. The *Oak Park Reporter* was an active paper that was started in 1887. Other local papers emerged in the 1880s and 1890s, with the *Oak Park Times* starting as a three-times-per-week effort and then decreasing to two and then to one time a week before being absorbed at the same time as the *Vindicator* into the *Oak Leaves* in January 1902.

Women's clubs and social organizations were also important, with groups such as the Left-at-Homes (founded in 1887), Travelers Club (1889) and Literary Club indicating their purposes in their names; the Nakama Club (1890) and the Nineteenth Century Club (1891), which became the Nineteenth Century Woman's Club after 1918, had broader social and educational aims, though some women refused to join because they feared that such secular clubs would weaken church-based organizations. Many of the same women joined charitable clubs, as well as social and church-related ones, with the Woman's

Hephzibah Home was founded in 1897 by Mary Wessels. She used her modest personal funds to develop the orphanage and purchased the Blackstone House on Lake Street in 1907. The current building was completed in 1928. *Courtesy of Hephzibah Children's Association.*

Benevolent Society being the earliest of them, founded in 1886. Members of that organization, as well as those in the Needlework Guild, had the making of clothes and blankets for needy families as their mission. Other organizations helped raise funds for Chicago's poorest families. Another, Hephzibah Home, was founded in 1897 as an orphanage.

While the cultural institutions were growing, infrastructure of the community was developing, mostly through private endeavors and without much township support, and matters of public safety became increasingly important to the residents of the community. Both police and fire protection were important issues but evolved in different ways and at different times. Whereas the response to fires had always been a matter of the commonweal, with volunteerism long the major part of this response, it is not surprising that the earliest step toward dealing with fires was through unofficial means.

Local men signed up to volunteer and dropped what they were doing when the bell was rung at Central School. Taking a hand-drawn cart with its modest water supply to the scene of the fire, they were often supplemented in manpower by whoever was around downtown at the time, usually hoping at best to contain the flames to the building in which the fire started. In the winter, faulty fireplaces and stoves were the primary causes of fires, but in the summer, "most of the work was confined to putting out prairie fires, sometimes as many as eight a day."[27] Even after more sophisticated equipment was acquired in the 1880s, and there was an official "hose-house," the firemen often arrived in time only to wet down the ashes. In spite of the need, the area was too sparsely settled and had no real central source of water. Thus, the combination of the availability and ability of volunteers to do the job, as well as the lack of physical resources, made it difficult to make progress in fighting fires until Cicero Township took the first steps in 1891 by creating fire departments with paid firemen supplementing the volunteers. By the end of the century, there was a concerted push to consolidate the firehouses in the community and move the main house toward the center of town.

Though there seem to have been unofficial night watchman activities at an early date, it was not until the late 1870s that the population growth and density made developing a police presence a real necessity. As the power to make arrests and transport prisoners to jail or courts involves legal issues, volunteerism was not a viable solution to dealing with such felons nor the victims or perpetrators of stabbings and shootings. The first official police officer was hired in 1878 and served for more than forty years. "Marshall Hacker," as he was known, worked twelve-hour days, and his duties included keeping the law, making arrests, transporting prisoners and caring for the

Above: The volunteer firemen of Fire Department No. 3 were dedicated local citizens, but the distance they had to travel to a fire by horse-drawn wagon made the need for additional fire stations for the growing village quite clear. *Courtesy of HSOPRF.*

Below: This photo of the Steiner Block was taken while the buildings along Lake Street were being lowered after paving. Mr. Steiner, who moved the post office to his building when appointed postmaster, is seen at the right. *Courtesy of HSOPRF.*

oil-fed streetlamps. He even had to extinguish the lamps at midnight.[28] The force was gradually augmented, but sixteen men were still all that covered all of the communities of Cicero, Berwyn, Austin and Oak Park by 1893.

James Scoville began to sell the property on the southern part of his holdings in the mid-1870s, and the new owners started subdividing it immediately. By 1878, the area had been subdivided into home lots as far south as Madison Street, though primarily in the western, or Oak Ridge, part. The population soared, reaching more than 1,800 by 1880, more than 4,500 by 1890 and then more than double to 9,353 by 1900, thereby creating greater demand for new schools, additional public safety measures, transportation options and infrastructure improvements.

As a sign of the times, there was much concern about the level of postal service, as well as the reality of the appointment as postmaster being a political plum. Two Oak Park men contended to replace the Republican-appointed postmaster in 1885. One of them was William Steiner, a Democrat, who had been so generous to his neighbors after the Chicago fire. Edwin Gale reported how he had spoken to a judge of some repute and, even though a Republican, decried the slanders against Steiner's character, helping to ensure that he would be fully considered.[29] Steiner was appointed and moved the post office to his building at Lake and Marion. He managed to upgrade the status of the local office to become the regional office for all of Oak Park, River Forest and Forest Park and instituted a carrier system of delivery. New mailboxes were installed at the railroad stations, pickup was put on a regular twice-daily schedule and locked boxes at the post office were also installed. In addition, he had built up the facility to include a staff of ten before being replaced by a Republican supporter of President William Harrison. His successor, Delos Hull, built a new brick building on Marion Street to both house an expanded post office and serve as the headquarters of his coal business. The vault was state-of-the-art fireproof, and the boxes had new-and-improved locks. As in nearly every community, various men were interested in holding political office, though few pursued the matter to such extremes as one of the Scoville relatives.

Charles Guiteau, a lawyer and the brother-in-law of George Scoville, James's brother, lived with his sister and her lawyer husband on Lake Street in the 1870s. Apparently more of a con man who seems to even have cheated the relatives with whom he lived, Guiteau sought various political appointments while practicing law in Chicago and wrote many letters to then United States secretary of state James Blaine and President James Garfield suggesting a variety of consular positions he could fill. When

Johnson's Restaurant and Sam Lee's Laundry were two of the many two-story wooden buildings along Lake Street in the early years of the village. The street numbers started with 1, at Harlem Avenue, and ascended as they moved eastward. *Courtesy of HSOPRF.*

neither responded, Guiteau moved to Washington, where he eventually shot the president on July 2, 1881. Though his brother-in-law tried to defend him in court after Garfield died, he was found guilty and hanged in June 1882.[30]

By the early 1880s, the Oak Park community boasted butchers, milliners, coal suppliers, a dairy, a baker, two drugstores, a stationer, a bootmaker/shoemaker, a hardware store, a jeweler and several general stores, as well as such service providers as a barber, a trucking business, a dentist, doctors, a photographer, an architect and an undertaker. One business, Peake's pharmacy, was more modern than others and boasted a hand-operated elevator. Most of the businesses were located along Lake Street and from Harlem eastward, though homes were interspersed among them. Other businesses were north or south of Lake Street, along what was Wisconsin or Marion, and a few were located closer to Oak Park Avenue and the railroad station that had been built through private subscription. Many buildings served several purposes, with retail establishments and some teashops on the first floor, professional offices on the second and sometimes apartments on the third floor of the newer brick buildings.

With the completion of Scoville's waterworks at his reservoir, and the construction of other, more modern, brick buildings at or around North

Boulevard and Oak Park Avenue, in addition to the continued increase of residential occupancy in the Ridgeland area, the businesses in the original wooden buildings near Lake and Harlem began to lose their competitive edge. With all of the growth, and new areas of retail activity, the lack of street signage became more of a problem for the community. In 1884, a newspaper article noted: "Subscriptions have been collected around the Village and on trains during the past week for the purpose of procuring some kind of signs for designating the streets."[31] The article mentioned the frustration of visitors in finding their way when many of the north–south streets' names changed from one end of town to the other, as three still do.

With the substantial growth of the population and its spread both eastward from Harlem Avenue and north and south from Lake Street, basic infrastructure needs became more apparent, especially in the areas of transportation and utilities. There were many false starts in developing additional rail service to the area, with franchises given by either Chicago or Cicero Township to would-be railroads that never actually laid any track. However, in 1881 one franchise provided that the Chicago Western Dummy Company would build a line on Randolph Street to Harlem Avenue. That line was opened a year later, with service south to the local cemeteries and with unreliable connections to a horse-drawn bus on Madison Street. During the Columbian Exposition, an additional temporary track was laid to the South Side of Chicago, with that line doing major business in bringing people down to the fair. Vestigial traces of the "dummy" line remain, most especially in the jog of the street and the rectangle of land that used to contain a station at Randolph Street and Lombard Avenue. "Dummy" line schedules were as unreliable as the connection to the bus until the entire operation was taken over by the Wisconsin Central Railroad in 1887.

Although there were several attempts to bring electrified rail service west from the city, they languished or failed to achieve funding through the 1880s. With the tremendous growth of residences in the area between Chicago Avenue and Madison Street in both Ridgeland and Oak Ridge in the late 1880s and early 1890s, electric street railways were developed to meet the needs of commuters and local users. Three major routes were constructed in the 1890s: along Roosevelt Road, Lake Street and Chicago Avenue, with various legs traveling east and west on Madison, Harrison and Randolph Streets to connect residents with both Chicago and downtown Oak Park. The original "dummy" steam railroad was also changed to an electrified street railway in 1897, and new schedules made trips available to and from Chicago, from early morning until late at night. Among several facilities where the cars were kept, one on Lake Street in Oak Park housed the horse-drawn cars and was designed in 1890 by Frederick Schock, the noted Chicago architect of major residential properties; two years later, he designed a larger barn for ninety cars there.

Street paving was another important part of the transportation issue, but one that was far more contentious than providing any form of public transportation. As reported years later by a member of the Cicero Township Board with a background of substantial community service and a long memory, an ordinance was made to regrade Lake Street from Oak Park Avenue to Harlem Avenue, with gravel, about 1880. The roadway was full of mudholes and often impassible, by either wagon or foot, but "[a] public meeting was held in the school house and people with mud holes in front of their premises denounced the improvement as unnecessary and extravagant and as something that would destroy the rural simplicity of the Village."[32]

Nonetheless, several of the major streets were curbed, graded and paved in the early 1890s, including Forest Avenue from Lake Street to Chicago

This photo shows the Madison Street streetcar, on the Chicago and Proviso Street Railway, one of the many electric lines that brought people around town until the competition of automobiles forced them out of existence. *Courtesy of HSOPRF.*

Above: This junction of the two alleys between Harlem Avenue and Marion Street was unpaved and a morass in rainy weather at the start of the twentieth century. The old wooden buildings were slowly replaced over the following two decades. *Courtesy of HSOPRF.*

Below: James Scoville's original Chicago Suburban Water and Light became part of a larger corporation in 1888, but the waterworks built in conjunction with the deep wells and reservoir on the property were still utilized until a municipal system was developed. *Courtesy of HSOPRF.*

Avenue, and Maple Street and Oak Park Avenue soon followed. But for the less business-oriented streets, placing blocks of cedar over graded streets was the preferred form of paving through the 1890s, until the rise of and increase in automobile travel made that system untenable—then sturdier bricks replaced the wooden blocks. Other signs of the times included the construction of the first major hotel, the Plaza, which opened in 1893 to accommodate people who wished to visit the Columbian Exposition easily yet have lodgings away from the crowds of the city.

The large sections of land had been subdivided, filled in slowly at first and then more quickly in the 1880s, though constructed lot by lot, with many homes built being the only ones on their blocks for a number of years. Small developers sometimes built two or three houses on speculation, sometimes occupying one and selling the rest to friends or relatives, and larger corner lots often contained larger homes than those on the interior of the block. Some of the large homes were imposing brick structures, housing families of the wealthier men who took the lesson of Chicago's fire to heart and had the resources to respond accordingly; other homes were workers' cottages of wood construction. A variety of architectural styles were adopted, including Italianate, Gothic Revival, shingle style and—increasingly in the later 1880s—American Four Square. About half of the residences received their water from the pipes run from the Scoville reservoir and artesian wells until 1888, when the operation was taken over by a new corporation.[33]

Many local residents purchased stock in this enterprise, called the Cicero Water, Gas and Electric Light Company, though control was maintained by Scoville and other prominent shareholders. Fire hydrants were part of the agreement, although only for Oak Park. Yet, until 1891, when a new well and pump were activated and meters installed, running water was not available to most homeowners, and many relied on their own wells, pumps and cisterns. As was described some years later: "The drinking water came from an outside well with chain-and-bucket pump, replacing one with a windlass and bucket. The wash water, collected from the roof, was stored in a cement-lined cistern under the kitchen."[34] In 1895, there were nine major wells on the old Scoville property, reaching more than two thousand feet in depth. The same company took over the responsibility of providing gas and electricity to the community after several firms that obtained the right to supply gas within Cicero Township failed to exercise their options. Under the new firm's direction, electricity became available for streetlighting in 1891, and the company obtained a franchise to provide gas for lighting and cooking the following year. A large-capacity gasworks

This major gasworks facility at Lombard Avenue and Garfield Street changed hands and names several times between its opening in 1893 and its closing in 1930. Coal was burned to create gas for home cooking and heating. *Courtesy of HSOPRF.*

was constructed in the southeast corner of Lombard Avenue and what was then called Harrison Place in 1893; the gasworks was a coal-burning facility with a huge tank that became a local point of orientation for decades to come.

Lighting for residential use came soon after the streetlights were electrified, but the lack of metering created a situation in which a flat rate was charged for those who converted from gas. Always the subject of much discussion about "wasteful habits" because of the flat rate, the utility shut down its power plant at midnight in partial response. Water became metered in the 1890s, again to conserve use but also to respond to citizen concerns about the level of taxation if a flat rate was used. The utility, which retained its name after 1897, provided gas, water and electricity but passed into the hands of a larger syndicate. Sewage and drainage were always closely related to water supply as an issue but were handled as a public utility rather than through private subscription. The first major trunk lines ran down Ridgeland and Oak Park Avenues and were made of brick. The feeder sewers were mostly of wood and became increasingly problematic over the next several decades.

These five attached homes on South Clinton Avenue, the E.F. Burton row houses, are typical of such groupings of the late 1880s and 1890s, with a continuous roofline and similar interior space but varied decorative elements and design on the exteriors. *Courtesy of the author.*

The population increase of the post–Chicago fire era continued, though at a less dramatic rate, in the later 1880s and 1890s. The areas from south of the tracks to Madison Street and north to Chicago Avenue and beyond began to fill in, with the large families of the era requiring several bedrooms on the second floor. The lots were smaller south of the tracks, with a typical frontage width of about forty feet, and the houses filled up most of the lots' widths. There were also groups of row houses, built on speculation, and though they had very little outdoor space, they were made of brick and had a full range of living spaces for a family. Their exteriors mimicked the larger single-family homes, "with the familiar towers, turrets and gables."[35] The backgrounds of the residents also became more diverse, though Oak Park was still primarily a community of white families of British and western European extraction.

Yet, there was already a very small community of African Americans and people of mixed races in the 1880s, early migrants from the southern states. They lived in or near the commercial core at the west end of town on Lake Street and just south of there on William (later Westgate) Street and down

Central School (later Lowell) was the first school built for the community, in 1859. It went through several expansions and later housed the District 97 administrative offices as well. This view looks east, from Park (later Forest) Street. *Courtesy of HSOPRF.*

to Randolph Street. A few others lived in the yet unsubdivided prairie area to the north, between present-day Augusta and Division Streets. Most of the small number of black men worked as railroad porters, coach drivers or stable hands, with women serving as maids and cooks and doing laundry.

A few of the early pioneers were entrepreneurs with diverse businesses. The most successful, Will Palmer, rivaled Austin and Scoville in the diversity of his enterprises: he was a teamster but also owned a scavenger service, purchased six homes and ran a boardinghouse. African American communal life was centered on religion, and in the earliest documented time, starting about 1887, a group of black Baptists met at Temperance Hall, as Henry Austin offered the facility to various congregations that didn't have their own churches.[36] After Austin's death in 1889, the congregation first met in a rented facility on Lake Street and then at the original building of Central School, a few blocks east. By the turn of the century, there were still fewer than one hundred African Americans in Oak Park, though the census figures were quite unreliable in reporting race or including people who lived in more sparsely settled areas of town. Many of the domestic workers who lived in their employer's homes may also have been undercounted.

With the growth of the community came greater needs for educational opportunities, and additions to existing buildings and new construction occurred throughout this period: a third wing of Central School was opened in 1880; the Ridgeland school was replaced by the William Beye School in 1896; two small buildings constructed in 1889 composed the Chicago Avenue School; two more buildings were the start of South or Washington Boulevard School in 1893; and Highland Avenue School was started in 1894 as a four-room building. Public kindergartens had not yet appeared before the turn of the century, though several were run in private homes. Offering a blend of education and child care, women with several children of their own, like F.L. Wright's wife, Catherine, had other children join their own for learning and play. At least one private school for young girls was the Starrett School, which was started in 1893 and met at the Scoville mansion on Lake Street.[37]

A separate high school was a priority for many, especially to provide college preparation for the sons of the upper-middle-class families who wished to have them move from commerce into the professions. Though the high school budget was not separated out from that of the elementary division,

This photo of a high school graduating class in the 1880s shows the level of formality associated with the event. While the young women wear full-length white dresses, the males are clad in suits and formalwear of different colors and styles. *Courtesy of HSOPRF.*

the names of all graduates are recorded. A principal of the high school was appointed in 1881, and the enrollment grew from forty-nine to well over one hundred in the following decade. By then, it was no longer deemed practical to try to expand the program at Central School, and a separate high school building was opened in December 1891 in the vicinity of the current high school. Fourth- through eighth-grade students used some of the space on the first floor until the new elementary schools were completed, and the older students were upstairs. The students of the senior class started a biweekly newspaper in 1894, and it soon became a monthly literary periodical. It has been noted that the school's reputation grew so quickly that, before 1900, many colleges accepted the school's diploma, or proof of graduation, as a basis of admission, without the need for an examination.[38]

In the *Third Annual Report of the Board of Education of School District Number One*, in 1897, the boundaries and borders of Oak Park were already clear, from Austin Boulevard to Harlem Avenue and from North Avenue to Twelfth Street, with five primary schools plus a high school under one board. Yet, one year later, local citizens were chafing under their limited ability to support the high school at a level beyond that allowed by the annual levy permitted under the law. Thus, a proposition was put to the voters to create a new high school district. As the smaller Proviso Township community of River Forest couldn't compete at the high school level and had been sending high school–age students to Oak Park as tuition-paying students for some years, the vote was to combine the high school populations of both Oak Park and River Forest. The voters approved the creation of the high school district by a wide margin, and a five-member high school board was elected in May 1899. The school was opened in 1900, in the same building but now under lease at an annual rental of $5,000 to the elementary school district.

Chapter 4

A VILLAGE IS BORN

The residents of Oak Park were not only seeing their community grow in numbers but also paying various assessments and taxes and supporting the services they wanted through subscription. The early township board and officers had important posts occupied by Oak Park men, but after the township charter was reincorporated and amended twice in the late 1860s, leadership was in the hands of a larger board with expanded powers and the ability to borrow for the purpose of making local improvements without having to wait to collect special assessments to pay for them. The percentage of Oak Parkers on the newly enlarged board, after the changes to its charter, was smaller than before, and the men from the east, or the Brighton Park area of the township, under the leadership of John McCaffery, began to consolidate power in 1869. The residents of Oak Park felt that they were not receiving their due share of Cicero Township resources, while they were paying the inflated salaries that the township board members were paying themselves and their cronies.

Residents became vexed at the level of taxation and what they perceived as the waste of their money on unnecessary public works projects that failed to respond to their needs. In particular, Oak Parkers were angered at the large expense for the town hall that was built in 1870–71 on the Township Square in Austin, which was like the kind of conspicuous public works being done in New York under Boss Tweed. And yet, while the local residents had to pay their share of the $600,000 that borrowing for the improvements in other areas had cost the township, no public works were constructed in the Oak

Park area with township tax funds, other than for some sewage drains.[39] The Oak Parkers led a fight for reform, displaying the same concentration and zeal that they used to fight the saloons, enabling them to defeat McCaffery and his friends at the local election of 1873.

Several of the new board members in office in the next decade were Oak Parkers, with such familiar names as Scoville, Herrick and Niles, joined by future leaders like John Blair, George Butters, John Lewis and Simpson Dunlop. Through the 1880s, they and their neighbors intently observed the

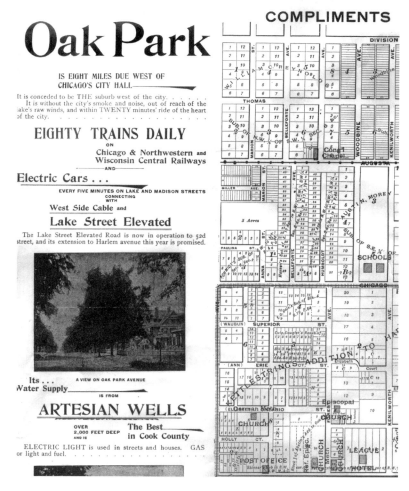

This detail of a large poster is an advertisement for Oak Park, almost a decade before the village gained independence from Cicero Township. The proximity to downtown Chicago, the transportation facilities and the pure water are all emphasized as selling points. *Courtesy of HSOPRF.*

annexing of more and more of the township into Chicago by action of the state legislature, by state law and through permitted elections. There was much sentiment for independence from the larger township, and the question of how to get support for such a move at the state level was a subject of many local political discussions. The factors in favor of such a move were the bad experiences with the machine-controlled township board, even though, at the end of the period, Oak Parker John Lewis was serving as the president of the board. Other factors included the desire to have local improvements decided exclusively locally, a wish to get the educational system free of the township and a general feeling among the active Oak Parkers that their values—including an antiliquor bias—were different from those of the other sections of the township, and they advertised their differences proudly.

There were local groups in Oak Park not found in other parts of the township, notably the Oak Park Improvement Association and a committee of the Nineteenth Century Club working to improve the quality of life by pushing for the enforcement of rules already on the books. Working to get state legislative support for disconnection from the township was not easy, and the thrust of lobbying efforts was for a law that would permit the division of incorporated towns rather than just the peeling off of parts for annexation to larger entities. The Oak Park leadership pushed hard for several years, and efforts were successful in June 1891. The law enacted allowed such divisions throughout the state, but the aim was to allow the division of Cicero Township. However, all votes to divide were put before the electorate of the entire township, rather than just the people in the areas under consideration.

The first election to test the possibility was a special election in 1895, when the voters had three related items on which to vote: one was to disconnect Oak Park and Ridgeland as a new town of Oak Park; another was to create a town of Berwyn with almost the same boundaries as it currently has; and the third was to create a town that approximates the current boundaries of Cicero, to be called Hawthorne. All of the measures lost, with voters in different sections having reasons not to let the others secede from the larger township. Attitudes toward either independence or annexation to Chicago varied both from area to area within the township and among different factions within each area. At the instigation of some Austin residents, a vote on the possible annexation of Austin to Chicago was held in 1898, and it, too, failed.

The Oak Parkers seemed to feel it unfair to help vote people into the city, when many others they knew opposed the move, so they tended to vote against the annexation. Frustrated by their lack of success, the successful and worldly civic leaders tried a different approach. Working with the leadership of Austin and Berwyn, these forces submitted three petitions to the county judge to permit disconnection from the township. The judge responded positively, special elections were held on December 20, 1898, and the voters in all three areas voted for disconnection by large majorities.[40] The result created a new township comprising the old Oak Ridge and Ridgeland, already united in a school district and many other ways. However, the enabling legislation hadn't mandated either a structure or the election of any officials, only the independence of the community from Cicero Township.

The leaders who had spearheaded independence created a committee of ten men to work on behalf of a smooth transition until an official government was formed, and they nominated candidates to serve as assessor, collector, supervisor and clerk the following week. Only one of the nominees, John Lewis, was one of the ten, but he was already an experienced member of the township board. The county court scheduled the election of the officers for only a month later, on January 17, 1899, and, as there was no other slate presented, the officers were elected. Public sentiment was almost unanimous in favoring a village form of government, and the officers set March 15 as the date for the election as to whether or not Oak Park was to become a village. The result was never in doubt, and preparations began at once to elect officers at an election the following month.

The celebration and preparations for an election turned out to be premature, as both a majority of the members of the Cicero Township Board and members of the Austin community combined to challenge the state law that had set up the possibility of disconnection in 1891. The Illinois Supreme Court met the day after the vote in favor of a village structure and declared the 1891 act unconstitutional. That decision undid all of the actions taken by the three new communities and put them back into Cicero Township and under the authority of its township board. That got the Oak Parkers and others who had voted against the annexation of Austin a year earlier angry that Austin had joined with the township in blocking the disconnection. So, when the Austin supporters of joining Chicago almost immediately requested a vote on annexation, the Oak Parkers turned out in force to vote Austin into the city. A separate vote to have all of Cicero Township annexed was roundly defeated.

Some of the Austin leadership joined the Cicero Township Board in challenging the constitutionality of the vote for annexation, and no actions were taken while the Illinois Supreme Court considered the matter. After the court acted swiftly and in October found the annexation vote appropriate

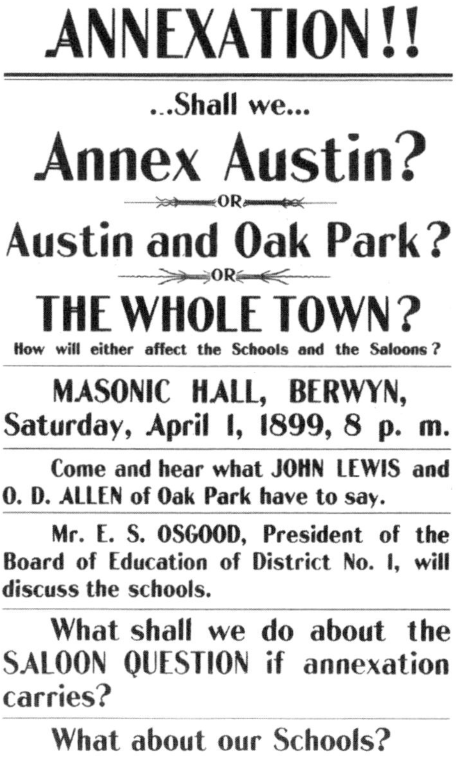

ANNEXATION!!

...Shall we...

Annex Austin?

⟫━━⟪OR⟫━━⟪

Austin and Oak Park?

⟫━━⟪OR⟫━━⟪

THE WHOLE TOWN?

How will either affect the Schools and the Saloons?

MASONIC HALL, BERWYN, Saturday, April 1, 1899, 8 p. m.

Come and hear what JOHN LEWIS and O. D. ALLEN of Oak Park have to say.

Mr. E. S. OSGOOD, President of the Board of Education of District No. 1, will discuss the schools.

What shall we do about the SALOON QUESTION if annexation carries?

What about our Schools?

This 1899 flyer raises the issues behind the upcoming annexation vote: should Oak Park stand on its own, and if so, what was the implication for the schools and for a saloon-free community? These were the concerns to be addressed at the scheduled meeting. *Courtesy of HSOPRF.*

and legal under the annexation procedures, Austin was incorporated into Chicago.[41] The Township of Cicero had to move from its town hall in Austin and transferred the offices to Oak Park, perhaps as a political gesture to keep the Oak Parkers loyal and minimize their dissatisfaction. However, that ploy carried no weight with the Oak Park citizens, who realized that the removal of a large bloc of Austinites from the township made a vote for division more likely, though a procedure had to be developed to withstand a legal challenge in the Illinois Supreme Court. The leadership appointed a committee to prepare a proposal that could be worked into a law that would permit the establishment of new communities.

What the committee developed was an amendment to the existing Cities and Villages Act, and with the help and support of Berwyn residents who also wanted their independence, the committee's representatives were able to secure passage in the 1901 session of the state legislature. Both communities immediately circulated petitions requesting a vote for disconnection from Cicero. The township questioned the constitutionality of the law under which it was applying. But this time, Judge Orrin N. Carter, the sole presiding judge of the Cook County Court, let the law stand, and the elections were called for November 1901. Both Berwyn and Oak Park decisively voted for separation, and the village of Oak Park was born, beginning with a population of 9,889, a mature educational system and five railways, as well as various other forms of public transportation.

Chapter 5

BECOMING OAK PARK

The first municipal elections of the new village of Oak Park were scheduled for less than six weeks after the granting of autonomy. With an active leadership in place, the fact that there were two competing slates for the new village board is surprising, and in reality there was only one significant issue on which the two groups disagreed. The process for setting up the government created eight voting precincts, and though there was no legislation that mandated either election of the board at large or by precincts, it became the one contentious issue. The men who had led the fight for separation from Cicero Township organized the Citizens Non-Partisan group and supported the election of the president, six trustees and the village clerk through voting at large; the other group, the People's Independent Party, favored having one of each of the officers nominated by each precinct, thus ensuring that all areas of the village would have representation.

The People's Independent Party won the first election in December 1901, and the first session of the board was held on January 2, 1902. Judge Carter declared Oak Park an official village later that month. The Oak Park Township was made a discrete entity on November 17, with the same borders as the village, and the voters elected the following officers: township supervisor, clerk, collector, assessor, five constables who served legal papers for the local courts and five justices of the peace who presided over cases involving violations of local ordinances and small civil suits. For many years, the clerk of the village and the clerk of the township were traditionally the same person.[42]

Many issues related to the separation from the larger Cicero Township needed prompt attention, including moving the township offices out of Oak Park, adjudication of financial issues, the access to and use of utilities, the independence of the schools and the need for a village hall headquarters for the uniformed officers. The president of the township board at the time of separation, John Lewis, already mentioned, though not elected to the new village board, had an important role in making things work. In his final report to the township board, Lewis had noted the problems with manure and ashes in the alleys and had also voiced support for a consolidation of the firehouses. But first came the relationship with the township.

The first president of the village, Allen S. Ray, submitted a report at the end of that first year, noting that "[n]egotiations are in progress with the City of Chicago and the Town of Cicero for a settlement of the amount due Oak Park in the transfer arising from the annexation of Austin to the City of Chicago, and from the separation of Oak Park from the Town of Cicero."[43] He further noted that the negotiations were complex and time consuming and involved large amounts of money. There were also several conflicting interests. Indeed, the complexity was such that Cicero Township continued to perform the property assessment and tax collections for Oak Park until the following year. Particularly vexing to all concerned was what might be Oak Park's share of the finances of the Education Office and the furniture and furnishings of the Township Office that had moved from Austin after its annexation. The stories about officers of the old township trying to seize furniture and the fight of the Oak Parkers to get compensation are humorous, though the *Oak Leaves* gravely reported: "On Wednesday, Clerk Brennan sent up a wagon to cart away the furnishings of the town office at 122 Oak Park Avenue…which Oak Park claims as a part of its share of the estate of the dismembered municipality, for which it is willing to pay the town a proper sum in the final settlement, but of the possession of which it does not propose to be divested without its own consent."[44] President Ray and several trustees let the Cicero Township people take some files, but the rest were put under lock and key and guarded by the police. This and other issues were resolved in the next two years, for the most part through peaceful negotiations.

One year after the new township had been established, the question of creating one township to include both Oak Park and River Forest was publicly aired. After a proviso township election about bond issues for rural roads, the editor of the *Oak Leaves* suggested that River Forest be incorporated into the Oak Park Township (though not the village). He opined: "There can be no question but that River Forest has much more in common with Oak Park

When Oak Park disconnected from Cicero Township, the first public work to be commissioned was a municipal building. Here the building is nearing completion in 1903. It housed the village government, the police force and the township government until the village administration began its move to a new building. *Courtesy of HSOPRF.*

than it has with the rest of the town of Proviso. It is already a part of the same high school district, and not only is its boundary contiguous to Oak Park, but its people are homogeneous with those of the larger village."[45] There was not much support for such a merger in either of the two new villages, and though the issue of some sort of merger was raised again many times throughout the years, it never came close to fruition.

Finding homes for the various arms of local government was a major priority of the new Oak Park government, though some of the public safety facilities were able to transfer from the township to the village under terms of the financial agreements reached, among them the old firehouse that had at an early date served only Ridgeland. At first the village government met at the Scoville Institute, until the new and substantial Municipal Building was completed on Lake Street at Euclid Avenue, a year after the government was seated. The new building contained the village chambers and various offices, as well as the police department and, soon, the Central Station of the Fire Department. When the building was completed, the township board met in the same council chambers as the village board of trustees and continued to do so for decades. The architect of the building, E.E. Roberts, was also the designer of the addition to the high school and of West Suburban Hospital. He had a very large practice, designing many homes in addition to these major public commissions.

Plans were also undertaken for a freestanding post office, with a major push from well-placed Oak Parkers despite the opposition of both the residents and businessmen of the west part of town and in River Forest to the proposed location. The classical structure was located just a block west of the Municipal Hall, at Lake Street and Oak Park Avenue, with its entrance on Oak Park Avenue. Its location also reflected the board's wish to concentrate the major public structures along the major east–west spine of the community, midway between the north and south boundaries and nearer to the geographic rather than the then population center of the village. To recognize the major patronage generated in the western part of town and the concerns of the business community, however, a substation was maintained on Marion, next to the old location.[46] The new building's cornerstone was placed with a full Masonic ceremony in 1905, and the building was opened a year later. Parcel post service was offered as early as 1913.

As the contract with Chicago Suburban Water and Light Company for streetlighting that had made Oak Park the first town to have electric streetlights was due to expire at the end of 1902, what to do next was an issue that had to be resolved quickly. Arc lights were installed and were maintained by the utility, burning until 1:00 a.m. The issue of a centralized heating system had already been settled in the year before the election for governmental separation but was still being finalized at that time. The Yaryan Company, a firm named after its inventor, held patents for a process for heating and supplying hot water to heat homes through a piping system. The company had obtained a franchise from Cicero Township but had not yet exercised it when it came up for renewal in 1901. Its appeal was that homes that participated in its program not only avoided the inconvenience and dirt associated with coal or oil furnace heating but also removed the need to have a heating system installed at all and kept the cost roughly the same as for heating with either traditional fuel.

Selecting a location both near the center of town and on the water table known to exist in the area, the firm sank a major well on property at North Boulevard and Euclid Avenue, just east of the original Scoville wells, and hired E.E. Roberts to construct a light and heating plant. Homes between East and Harlem Avenues and Chicago Avenue to Madison Street could sign up, and homes built on empty lots in the area at a later date were hooked up under the same terms made available to the original subscribers, at prices then current. Continuous heat was provided twenty-four hours a day through the heating season, which ran from September 15 to May 15. Streetlighting was also contracted with the Yaryan Company at this time,

The Yaryan plant provided heat to the homes in the central area of town from its opening at North Boulevard and Euclid Avenue in 1901 through its closing in 1958. Only heat for the upper floors was needed by Yaryan's customers. *Courtesy of HSOPRF.*

and the firm agreed to provide lighting that would be on all night for $49.50 per light per year. The system remained in use until 1958.

Resolving the access to water was different, with more players competing to serve as suppliers, as well as constant agitation on the part of some to create a totally village-owned municipal water system. Contracts with the Chicago Suburban Water and Light Company had been renegotiated through the late 1880s and 1890s before the company was sold to private investors in 1905. Water purity was always a topic of local discussion, with fear of typhoid and suspected unsanitary conditions, so the village finally acted and built a municipal water plant to process the Lake Michigan water it obtained from the city. The contract is an early example of both the reliance of the village on Chicago and its desire for independence: "On December 3, 1908, a contract was signed by the Mayor of Chicago and the President of Oak Park, on behalf of their respective communities, by which Oak Park has the perpetual right to take an unlimited supply of water from the City of Chicago at the lowest rate which said City of Chicago shall make to any customer."[47] That relationship remains on the books today, though many changes were made to the rate and additional mains and pumping stations were created in the village. Improving the streets was an issue with less universal support than supplying pure water and adequate heat and light, as evidenced in the 1903 *Annual Report of the Village*. The report noted that many of the citizens on the streets who were deemed most in need of sewer, gutter or paving work opposed the assessments when requests for such levies were made to the county court that had to approve them.

Two other services for the public were also changed at this time. Telephone service was a comparatively new concept when the village was created, as the first village phone had been installed in 1895. There were two competing companies for a few years, but the Chicago Bell Company had absorbed the local independent one soon thereafter. The popularity of phone service in residential buildings matched that of businesses. There were about one thousand phones in use at the time of disconnection from Cicero, and soon the utility was moved into its own building. The steam railroad system disappeared at this time, having outlived its usefulness. The old "dummy" line acquired by the Lake Street Elevated Company was no longer popular or necessary and was abandoned by the new owners. The village forced the company to remove the tracks and the stations in 1904.

Two additional issues faced by the young community related to the Scoville Institute and the high school. The former had been set up with James Scoville's gift providing that the institute should not collect a tax nor charge anyone to use the library. However, rental and entertainment fees could not keep up with the cost of running the operation, nor could donations support the level of book buying for both adults and children. With nine thousand volumes, the library was so popular that it attracted about twenty thousand visitors. A lot of sentiment for greater support of the library was generated, with organized fundraising and pleas for public backing. A citizens group petitioned the village to approve a public tax to support the library part of the institute, rather than voiding Scoville's intent. The citizenry approved a two-mill tax by a resounding five-to-one margin, and the Oak Park Public Library trustees took office in April 1903. Under the agreement made between the library board and the trustees of the institute, the library utilized most of the space in the building, while the cost of operating the building was shared by the library and institute boards.[48]

Later that year, recognizing that so much had changed in the schools since they had originally been built and named, and partially to recognize the new community and its level of aspirations, the school board voted to rename the school buildings after major literary figures. The original Central School became Lowell, North became Holmes, South became Emerson, Augusta became Whittier, Sixty-fourth became Hawthorne and Highland became Longfellow. Only the more recently named Beye School, honoring a beloved educational leader, kept its name.

However, by the time the village was formed, enrollment had increased sufficiently so that a new high school building was a major topic of discussion. There was talk of an addition, with labs, space for physical education, shops

This building stood on the south side of Lake Street at East Avenue and was the first home of the high school after it left the all-grades Central School in 1891. The new school was completed in 1907, and the old building was later home to Bishop Quarter School, a Catholic military school. *Courtesy of HSOPRF.*

and a lunchroom to the south, where the noise from trains and streetcars wouldn't matter as much. However, it was finally decided that an addition would be a temporary expedient and that constructing a new and larger high school was inevitable. It took several years, until the building was dangerously overcrowded and space was being rented elsewhere for both classrooms and athletics, while citizens argued both finances and, more passionately, the appropriate location. Finally, in 1904, the voters decided to accept the school board's recommended location between East and Scoville Avenues, on the north side of Lake Street, and the first part of the building was opened in 1907.

Thus, within five or six years of the creation of the village of Oak Park, and in spite of the still much greater concentration of both businesses and residences in the western part of town, the fact that the municipal building, post office, high school and major utilities were all located in the same central area indicated the belief that it was only a matter of time until the population would grow to fill in the entire area within its boundaries. By the time the major institutions and structures of government and business were in place, about 1907, the population of the village exceeded sixteen thousand.

The elections of the first decade set the tone for the first years of the village's political life: the main components included nonpartisan slates rather than slating by the traditional political parties, few terms for the president and trustees before opting not to run (with the clerk often staying in office much longer) and freedom jealously guarded from outside interference. The young village had a political advantage over most other new and yet-to-be-born suburbs, as mentioned previously: all of the main taxing bodies (except the high school, which also includes River Forest) were and remain coterminous, including all of Oak Park and only Oak Park. That was also true of the village, township, public library district, elementary school district and, later, the park district. The community was fortunate in that it also had the support of Henry Austin Jr., an Illinois state senator from 1902 to 1922.

Chapter 6

GROWING PAINS

As the village became more and more popular as a place for Chicago businessmen to live, as the reputation of its schools grew and as it increasingly became a center of commerce for the emerging western suburbs, there was a substantial demand for housing. Both the "magnificent double rows of maples and elms that line the wide highways of beautiful Oak Park" and the availability of well-structured services were extolled in generating new development.[49] The boosters were successful and helped generate so much activity that the members of the real estate sales community formed their own organization, with a son of Edwin Gale, Thomas Gale, as president.

Three different types of residential growth occurred at that time: larger homes in the area north of Chicago Avenue and east of Oak Park Avenue, smaller ones south of Madison Street and multiple-unit buildings primarily along major arteries. The earliest multiple-unit buildings were residential hotels that contained both apartments with public spaces such as a dining room and a social hall and on-site management, making these buildings the forerunners of today's senior independent living buildings. Two-flats were more numerous in the early years of the twentieth century and caused greater anxiety among the owners of traditional single-family homes. Dire warnings of the end of suburban living and urban encroachment and decay appeared in the newspapers, with rhetoric as negative as if they were large tenements: residents would have no access to healthy nature, the air would be foul and unhealthy, disease would spread and property values would drop. The lack of green space, particularly the want of a front yard at most of the two-flats, was especially irksome to homeowners.

Typical of two-flats built throughout Oak Park in the early years of the twentieth century, the uniformity of façade and continuity of details on both the first and second floor is part of the attempt to make the building look like the single-family homes around it. *Courtesy of the author.*

In the initial land sale of the 1830s, a large portion of the property south of what became Madison Street had been purchased by one real estate speculator, Augustus Garrett. His holdings covered most of the area from Harlem east to Ridgeland and between Madison and what is now known as Roosevelt Road. The area changed hands several times and was not considered ready for development until Seward Gunderson and Thomas H. Hulbert purchased and held most of it for a number of years, until they felt that the time was ripe. The area was subdivided into much smaller lots than were found across the center middle of the village, with extra north–south streets inserted from Madison Street to Roosevelt Road. Then, both Gunderson and Hulbert began building houses on the area they had divided. The primary lot size of 37.5 feet wide in the first group of houses and then 40.0 feet wide in the second was both shallower and sometimes narrower than found elsewhere, due to the number of extra intervening streets in the area. The prices, from just over $3,000 to about $4,000 for the average home, were aimed at a new market of immigrants and workers of a somewhat lower income than were the prices of the houses to the north.

In the years between 1905 and 1920, Seward Gunderson built, financed and sold about six hundred homes, with a large number of the Oak Park residences in the two areas on the south side and surrounding the street that bears his name. The homes sold briskly, almost as soon as they were available for sale. Several of the families who were long involved with real estate worked with Gunderson. For example, the James family started out as subcontractors under Gunderson and then moved into the selling of real estate in their own businesses. Gunderson took on marketing practices that

This view of several homes in the Gunderson Historic District shows how the basic form remains, in spite of the closing in of porches and other minor changes. *Courtesy of the author.*

later proved successful elsewhere in Chicago and beyond, taking out building permits for many houses at once, buying materials in bulk and constructing many of essentially the same house within the same subdivision. However, his level of advertising went beyond that of many of his competitors, with weekly ads in both the local and the Chicago newspapers. Many of his ads and several pamphlets were directed at city dwellers, urging them to trade the problems of Chicago for healthier air, better schools and ease of transportation to downtown.

He also played on both status and economic issues in pushing the advantages of homeownership over renting. The newspaper responded to his patronage by reporting on recent sales in the Gunderson subdivision, including the name and occupation of each new owner.[50] The area filled in so rapidly that one of the local papers was able to gush how the area had changed from "one large prairie, with the blue grass waving in the breeze. Now the whole territory is dotted with handsome residences."[51] And although there was growth throughout Oak Park, it was primarily the Gunderson and Hulbert developments that caused the population to jump from 16,327 in 1907 to 20,911 in 1910.

Also, and much commented on at the time, Gunderson made a major point of moving his family into one of the homes in the middle of the subdivision, while his brother moved into another one across the street. Both

Seward Gunderson's ads stressed the many features found in the homes in his Oak Park subdivision. The homes are American Four Square, with a variety of porches and other details to individualize them. *Courtesy of HSOPRF.*

families became active in Oak Park organizations and society and attempted to lead the new residents toward appropriate middle-class conduct by example and direction. Gunderson's youngest daughter was later to report how her father instructed the buyers who had come from Europe and were not fully Americanized by telling the woman to wear hats instead of babushkas, that they should carry a purse when appearing in public and that it was important that their entire family attend church together on Sundays. The developer even encouraged the new homeowners to bring their parents to the home "closing" so they would absorb the etiquette for suburban visits.[52]

While the Gundersons were developing the area south of Madison Street with solid and well-built but fairly standardized homes, Frank Lloyd Wright and his Prairie School colleagues were filling in the already developed area north of Lake Street and between Oak Park and Harlem Avenues with custom-designed homes for prosperous and adventuresome clients. Most of the homes that Wright designed for his major clients were built between 1901 and 1909, when he left Oak Park and his family. However, members of his studio and close followers continued to work in his style or form for the next decade or so, increasingly in the north, as settlement occurred in the area up to Division Street.

We have seen that Gunderson and Hulbert's clients were people moving up into the middle class, but those who hired Wright, Charles White, E.E. Roberts or G.W. Maher were already men of substance and usually active within the community. For example, when the Oak Park Chamber Music Association was founded in 1904, of the ten trustees of the organization were Arthur Heurtley, Nathan Moore and W.H. Winslow, all men who had their family homes designed by Wright. Not surprisingly, members of these

This view through the canopy of majestic elm trees frames the Frank Lloyd Wright–designed William E. Martin House of 1903. The arch of the trees was long one of the great natural treasures of the community but steadily fell prey to Dutch elm disease. *Courtesy of the Village of Oak Park.*

and other affluent and socially prominent families were active on the boards of many other organizations, church councils and social clubs. Not many of those leaders lived in the southern part of town, nor did their less affluent neighbors feel that they were being treated right by the establishment.

In spite of de facto aldermanic-type elections, the citizens south of Madison continued to feel that they were not getting public works and other services commensurate with the taxes they paid. Petitions circulated in both 1910 and 1911 requesting a vote for annexation to Chicago and were supported by the various local businesses and other groups, but annexation was defeated in both elections. But another issue remaining from the creation of the village, one that didn't split along regional lines, was whether or not to have a professional manager administer the village's business and supervise its staff. There were national organizations making information available and advocating a village manager form of government, and the issue was hotly debated in the election of 1915, along with continued discussion of whether to have precincts select candidates for the board. The Primary Association nonpartisan slate advocated the change to the village manager form, and the New Citizen's Party opposed it. The former group won in April that year, but members were unable to move the community to institute the change.

The village was not only growing but also diversifying in more ways than just socioeconomic class. By the end of the first decade of independence from Cicero Township, all of the major churches along Lake Street had been built, as had many others throughout the village. The Congregationalists were the largest, most affluent and most influential of the Protestant denominations

Frank Lloyd Wright stated, "Unity Temple is my contribution to modern architecture." It was dedicated in 1909 and is the home of the Unity Temple Unitarian Universalist Church of Oak Park. Unity Temple Restoration Foundation exists to preserve and restore this national landmark. *Courtesy of Lisa Kelly and Unity Temple Restoration Foundation, with all rights reserved.*

in the early twentieth century and had established six Congregationalist churches by 1906. The Methodist, Episcopal and Presbyterian churches were later joined by the Unitarians and Universalists in 1909, when Wright built what would become his world-famous Unity Temple on sites along Lake Street and mostly designed by well-known and often local architects. The Baptists and the Lutherans built large churches nearby, and several large Methodist churches and other, mostly smaller congregations were also added during these growth years. Many were later merged or closed as population changes and ease of transportation made consolidation desirable. Most of these many congregations opened their buildings with only a minimum of "not in my backyard" objections, but other minority groups had a rougher path to establishing themselves in the village.

Though Oak Ridge Roman Catholics had worshiped in River Forest for many years, and those in Ridgeland were part of the same parish as their coreligionists in Austin, there was no building in Oak Park for them until St. Edmund's Parish was organized in 1907 and began planning to construct a church. More than token opposition arose to the erection of the proposed building, though several important community leaders voiced their support. After the first mass was held in the stable on the Scoville estate in July 1907, the congregation worshiped in rented space until the building was completed in 1910. John Farson helped support the congregation, too, as he was a major supporter of almost all Oak Park causes and a liberal and charitable individual. Always seen as far more broad-minded than his neighbors, he allowed parishioners of St. Edmund's to use his home for a benefit to raise funds to build the first Catholic church in the "predominantly Protestant community."[53]

Though that construction went fairly smoothly on a main street, Oak Park Avenue, pronounced animosity and public accusations in the press emerged when the archbishop of Chicago attempted to buy a site for the Ascension Parish farther south late in 1907. The owner of the Phoenix Clubhouse on the 600 block of South Scoville Avenue had been renting this facility to Grace Church for outreach work, and the rector of Grace claimed to have a lease that would let him stay, in spite of the owner having sold it to the Catholic archdiocese. The rector claimed that no religious prejudice was involved when he opposed the sale, but the tone of correspondence with the seller suggested otherwise. One letter to the seller, Mr. Flitcraft, was particularly damning. As Reverend Shayler of Grace wrote: "Without disparagement or prejudice I am sure you can see that it will be better for you, for the property, for the neighborhood, for Oak Park, if we use it for Grace Church than if the R.C.s get it. You know the quality of their people and one glance at a used parochial school or public building of theirs will tell you what would happen to your building and neighborhood if they lease it."[54] Eventually, after some time in the rental, the Roman Catholic congregation was able to complete its building five years later.

St. Edmund Parish is the oldest Roman Catholic church in Oak Park. Its first pastor, Monsignor John Code, served for almost fifty years. Pictured is the sanctuary as originally designed and completed in the 1920s. *Courtesy of Archives of Mary Wentland of St. Edmund Parish.*

After several years at Temperance Hall and at a rented storefront, the small African American congregation of Oak Parkers purchased a lot on Chicago Avenue, between Cuyler and Ridgeland Avenues, for $600 and prepared to build its own church in 1902. The village issued a building permit, and a deacon of the congregation publicly thanked "our many friends, both white and colored, who have so kindly assisted us."[55] However, the reaction of the neighbors was so hostile that the village rescinded the permit. The Cuyler neighbors offered to buy the property for $2,000, and rather than fight and try to worship in a hostile environment, the church elders accepted the offer. Feeling that it would be more comfortable for everyone if their church was nearer the center of the black community, they purchased a lot for $1,000 from one of their congregants who had been given it by her white employer. The property was located on William (later Westgate), near Marion Street. They broke ground in June 1905, and the brick building, Mount Carmel Baptist Church, was dedicated on November 19 of that same year.

Members of a black Masonic lodge aid the congregation at the laying of the cornerstone at Mount Carmel Baptist Church on June 18, 1905. The building was complete and dedicated on November 19 that year. *Courtesy of HSOPRF.*

Not all members of the community were like the Cuyler neighbors; in addition to helping out and supporting the building of St. Edmund's, Farson also stepped in when the African American community that was still concentrated near Harlem and Lake attempted to build its church. Farson's contribution was a substantial $500, and other whites joined the black Baptist churches of Chicago in support of the building fund. Equally important as financial help was the public support of such men as the nationally known white minister Reverend William Barton, the longtime pastor of First Congregational Church. Not only did Barton speak out in favor of the black community having its church, he also hosted Booker T. Washington as a speaker at his church, using the admission proceeds to benefit the new Mount Carmel Baptist Church. Ironically, the one-dollar admission charge was too expensive for many of the members of Mount Carmel.[56]

Other groups, including the Nineteenth Century Club, sponsored forums and talks on improving race relations in Oak Park and beyond as early as 1904. Yet a few years later, the editor of the *Oak Leaves* was writing that a new homeland should be created out of Mexican territory and that American blacks should be sent there. His was a minority voice yet hardly a private one, writing in the major newspaper in town. Thus, there was both acceptance and support of the rights of the African American community, but probably not much more direct interaction than in other integrated communities, other than when black baseball teams played in Oak Park against local white teams and through minimal interaction among children in school. Certainly, almost no socializing occurred across racial lines.

Not all charitable institutions received the same welcome, either, with varying degrees of "not in my backyard" feelings coming into play. That was particularly true with regard to the creation of the two hospitals in the community, both of which were founded in this era. Though the village had created a department of health in January 1905 and appointed a board of health composed of three doctors, followed by an ordinance that set forth health regulations, no hospitals were located west of Garfield Park, and only a tiny converted building in Maywood offered any kind of medical care.

As a result, several citizens in the newly formed village began to talk about the need for medical care. Those most interested, including Dr. J.W. Tope, held a meeting at the Scoville Institute in 1904, with the express purpose of founding a modern hospital. They called themselves the Oak Park Hospital Association, rejecting offers of cooperation from forces in Austin and wanting instead a locally controlled facility. The association took an option on a property in a growing residential area a few blocks north of the high school and tried to enlist public support. There were citizens who favored the project, but vociferous opposition to a hospital in their neighborhood prompted the printing of flyers and a door-to-door campaign against the placing of the facility. As a result, the citizenry voted the project down in 1905. Also finding little support for the facility to be controlled by Oak Parkers, the association was disbanded. Dr. Tope persevered and contacted the Mercy sisters of Montreal, knowing of their success in founding and running other hospitals. After they agreed to take on the project, Dr. Tope raised $15,000 locally.[57]

Instead, the sisters agreed to immediately erect a hospital here and put $100,000 into the building and its equipment. The site selected was near the west end of town, just south of Madison Street. To counter fears and the same kind of opposition that had greeted the earlier plan, the hospital was bounded by alleys to minimize contact with the surrounding properties. Still fearful of the project, nearby residents dropped their opposition to the issuance of a building permit only when the hospital board agreed that the hospital would handle neither infectious nor contagious diseases. Ground was broken on April 6, 1906. The public responded very well to the handsome building and quickly recognized it as an asset. Private local fundraising endowed various spaces, and the building was dedicated a year later. A nursing school and housing for them was started, and the official name of the institution became the Oak Park Hospital and Training School for Nurses of the Sisters of Misericorde.

The rapid growth of the Oak Park population and the large area served by Oak Park Hospital suggested the need for another facility farther east within a couple of years. Rather than businessmen, a group of physicians, representing Oak Park, Austin and the immediate western suburbs, incorporated in April 1911 as the West Suburban Hospital Association, with the intention of erecting a major edifice on the current site. Again, there was opposition from local residents, who put their concerns in writing and asked the village board to deny a building permit. The residents cited their belief that the presence of a large building, the care of the sick, a fear of contagion and other factors would hurt their property values and diminish the desirability of the area as a residential neighborhood. The board sided with the residents and denied the permit.

The association pursued legal action, and the court moved to have the village grant the permit. The neighbors formed an organization to fight back, bringing their case to the Illinois Supreme Court, but lost on the technicality that the appeal had not been filed in a timely manner. Additional land was acquired, and this hospital opened in February 1914, with a special orientation

This view shows the original entrance of Oak Park Hospital, founded in 1907, now owned by the Wheaton Franciscan Sisters and administered as Rush Oak Park. There was tremendous resistance to both local hospitals, as neighbors feared contagion and the loss of property values. *Courtesy of HSOPRF.*

toward obstetrics. Once again, contagious diseases were not to be handled, and mental patients were also excluded. Both hospitals had been cooperating with the department of health since they were founded, but the relationships became more regularized and official when the village appointed the first health commissioner and an advisory medical staff in 1916. The first school nurse was appointed the same year, followed by a major increase to six after the national influenza epidemic of 1918, with four nurses funded by the board of education and two funded by the high school board.

Although there had been scattered and mostly small women's charitable organizations in the community since the Civil War, many of the major ones hit their stride in this period. The thrust of the earlier Hephzibah Home and other groups was to serve children. The Oak Park and River Forest Day Nursery was organized in 1912, its founders being members of the Nineteenth Century Club. Two important groups were the Oak Park Hospital Auxiliary, founded in 1907, and West Suburban Hospital Service Guild, founded in 1914, both of which had the mission of helping provide free hospital care for those who couldn't afford it. The Infant Welfare Society was organized in 1916 to help mothers raise healthy children. These and other charities were helped by the Economy Shop, which used the proceeds of its sales of donated goods to provide support.

Given all of the growth of public buildings, homes, churches and the clubhouses of charitable and fraternal organizations, obvious indications that the community was having growing pains included the repeated and sometimes passionate twin issues of the naming of the streets and the numbering of the buildings. Names had changed since the early 1870s, when Harlem Avenue was called Oak Park Avenue; the present Oak Park Avenue had different names north and south of Lake Street; various streets that ran north and south were named after states; and most of the other streets were named after the family members of such founders and early developers as Kettlestrings, Scoville, Austin and others.

Slowly, and at first by private subscription, street name signs began to appear in the mid-1880s, and a local druggist, Orin Peake, produced the first registry of citizens and their addresses. By the early 1890s, the system of naming the east to west streets was fairly established and uniform, following almost all Chicago street names all the way west through Oak Park. Yet the numbering ran from Harlem eastward when the village was formed, evoking arguments about whether to have street names or numbers on the major north–south arteries; also debated was the need for street naming and numbering to change between north and south, as in Chicago.

That these controversies were ongoing is evident by an impassioned letter to the editor in the *Oak Leaves* in April 1902 titled "Street Names Again." The writer starts with the disclaimer that he knew the editor to be "innocent of any desire for annexation, and yet I know you are fostering the spirit of annexation by urging the naming and numbering of our streets in conformity with the system (or lack of system) adopted from Chicago."[58] He goes on to defend the names of the arteries and notes that names like Ridgeland are more harmonious than Sixty-fourth Street. He then fulminates against a dividing line with streets numbered in ascending order in both directions from Madison, as well as asking why only Madison rather than any other street. He then uses a picturesque analogy of counting on our fingers and reminds us that we start at one end or the other, not with the middle finger. Finally, in a burst of local patriotic fervor, he ends with: "If we make Oak Park a part of Chicago in everything but name, we shall soon lose even the name. Let Oak Park be Oak Park, one and indivisible, great and ineffaceable."[59]

The division at Madison was put into place, but the direction of numbering and whether to continue the Chicago numbering west of Austin Boulevard remained issues for another decade. For a while, the businesses tended to use Chicago numbering on the streets that continued from Chicago, though many of the homes displayed numbers that were unique to Oak Park. Finally,

Strickland's and Lyon and Healy were two of the chains of stores that graced Marion Street, just south of Lake Street, for several decades. Strickland's was more local and specialized in home delivery. *Courtesy of HSOPRF.*

with many dissatisfied with the decision, in early 1915 the village officially set the system of using the tracks just south of Lake Street as the dividing line between north and south (except on Austin Boulevard), starting the east–west numbering at Austin and setting out requirements for the display of numbers on each building.

The business community had been slowly shifting from the Harlem to Marion area along Lake Street in the late 1890s, though the presence of the waterworks and the Yaryan heating plant limited growth south of Lake Street. But the erection of the building for the Avenue State Bank on the southeast corner of Oak Park Avenue and Lake Street in 1899 had really signaled a move toward the area. In addition, the 1905 opening of the Masonic Building that E.E. Roberts designed brought new stores, offices and public space to the corner of Lake Street and Oak Park Avenue, located diagonally across from the post office. In the teen years of the 1900s, the opening of such major stores as William Y. Gilmore's and Grable's made the section of Oak Park Avenue just south of Lake Street into a fashionable shopping area, a position it held until Lake Street near Harlem Avenue regained the leadership in the mid-1920s. Marion Street, south of Lake Street, also grew in importance at that time. Gilmore's opened in 1917 as a dry goods store and then grew into a larger business, with branches in other communities.

Also during the early years of the twentieth century, the often large homes near the railroad tracks were gradually being replaced with new businesses and larger commercial buildings, while, much more slowly, additional retail businesses opened to cater to the growing residential areas south of the tracks and in the Gunderson/Hulbert subdivisions. Seeing an opportunity to generate business among the new residents of the area, Suburban Trust and Savings Bank opened in 1912, later building its own anchor structure at Oak Park Avenue and Harrison Street. Soon, grocers, shoemakers, bakeries and the other standard businesses that catered to families were opening on Madison Street, South Oak Park Avenue and, to a lesser extent, Harrison Street. Only a few businesses were on Chicago Avenue and more on Lake Street near Austin Boulevard at this time, but all of these grew in the next decade.

An unofficial Business Men's Organization had been formed in 1895, with the specific purpose of stopping retailers from extending too much credit to customers who might not then be able to pay their bills. The group was then incorporated in 1905, with close to two hundred members, serving as the core of the larger group that later became the chamber of commerce. Many of these same businessmen also became founding members of the local chapters of such national groups as the Rotary Club. A local real estate board was founded in 1917, another sign of the growth of the community.

Not only did the citizens of Oak Park do business here, commuters from Austin, other parts of Chicago, Cicero, Berwyn, Maywood and beyond also utilized the growing shopping centers. The availability of many transportation alternatives made that possible, as one could access the village through any of the following: the Chicago Avenue, Lake Street, Oak Park Avenue, Madison Street or Metropolitan Elevated systems, as well as the Twelfth Street Line and the Northwestern and Great Western Railroads. In addition, as early as 1912, Murphy's Livery and Garage was offering day and night transportation in the village, while Oak Park Taxi was advertising "When Coming From Chicago—Get Off at Ridgeland Avenue and Take a Taxi."[60] One enterprising man, Wilbert Haase, was the first to try operating a "jitney" cab the length of Oak Park Avenue in 1915. His service included the entire length of the street and was such that you could hop on anywhere; it only lasted three days, having sixty-eight fares on the last day and not covering the cost of gasoline.

With the spread of the town and dispersal to the farthest corners, the old ways of dealing with the postal, police and fire services were increasingly antiquated by 1915, when the population had grown by another nine thousand people in five years, to twenty-nine thousand people. The three

When the first motorized mail delivery truck was brought into service in 1915, it was able to cover the same route that had been serviced by three horses and wagons. *Courtesy of HSOPRF.*

horses and wagons that had been collecting the mail were retired, and one car and driver were able to both make all the collections and do parcel post deliveries. Protection from catastrophic fires became more important as the population both spread and intensified. The need to reach the far corners of sparsely settled parts of town was different from the need to contain fires in the homes that were so close to one another on small lots on the narrower streets, thus calling for quicker access and more stations.

The first chemical and hose wagon was purchased with funds raised by the volunteer fire association of Ridgeland, which worked out of the old station at Lombard Avenue and Lake Street, with the promise that the equipment would stay at that station. Following the lead of the postal service, the village retired the horses and old wagon in 1915 and retrofitted the hook and ladder to a car. The south part of the village was served by a station at Harrison Street and East Avenue as early as 1913 and remained in use until replaced by a new station at Garfield, while the north side got its station on Augusta Street and Harvey Avenue in 1916. At the same time, as the northern station was also on the east side of the village, the original Ridgeland Station was closed and its equipment sent to the Central Station.

In the early days of the new village, there were about a dozen police officers, and reportedly one policeman patrolled Washington Boulevard daily, with two men on Sunday, looking for bicycle speeders who showed off by racing down

Washington Boulevard in excess of the eight-mile-per-hour speed limit. But more serious matters demanded law enforcement attention with the increase of population and the loss of knowledge of who lived where.[61] With the development of a central police station in the new municipal building, new forms of professional practice were instituted. Mandatory shooting practice was started in 1906, and a new switchboard was installed.

With the increase in population in both the village and the Austin neighborhood of Chicago, the Oak Park police chief was complaining of an inadequate and antiquated force by the time he submitted his report for the year 1911. He noted that there were only sixteen members, whereas national standards called for twenty-two, and that motorized vehicles and a fingerprinting system were needed, among other budgetary requests. He also noted the ease of criminal access and getaway on public transportation. The chief documented 453 arrests that year, though 197 were for violations of state motor vehicle laws and only 51 were felonies. His report gave a full list of the types of crimes, including the section on state misdemeanors: adultery, bastardy, cruelty to animals, wife abandonment, making threats to kill and violations of the oleomargarine law.[62] Clearly, much of the total crime was not a threat to life or property, but the small force was quite busy and in need of technological updating. Most of what the police chief requested came into being over the next few years, starting with the replacement of horse-drawn police wagons.

The growing community, which had already shown its commitment to music while it was still part of Cicero Township, sprouted new organizations and the structures to house them in the immediate years after disconnection. The first, and largest, structure was the Warrington Opera House, with seats for 1,500 patrons and designed by the extremely busy E.E. Roberts in 1902. But as the demand for opera was modest and the season short, the building soon hosted plays, concerts and other entertainments as well. By 1910, comedies, melodramas and classical theater took place for individual performances or extended runs.

Within a few years, movies started to be more than a novelty, and the Playhouse Theater was built around the corner from the Warrington. In addition, the Oak Park Theater tried to maximize profits by hosting both movies and vaudeville shows. Blue laws were then in effect, and each time the voters had a chance to consider whether or not to allow the theaters to show movies on Sunday, the naysayers won. Other theaters and social halls followed in the 1910s and beyond, and new music and theater groups joined or replaced those that were active in the 1880s and 1890s.

Most popular for some years was the amateur municipal band, started by a local craftsman, Joseph Farr, in 1914, with twenty-four local players who met at the municipal hall, paying no rent. As the park district refused to let the group offer its free concerts on any of the district's grounds, it played at Central School and other public locations. It also accompanied the six hundred Oak Park women who marched in the Chicago suffragette parade to celebrate Illinois' granting women the vote in local elections.[63] But professional concerts continued in the various venues, with Frederick Stock and the full Chicago Symphony Orchestra giving a series of four concerts at the high school auditorium in the autumn and winter of 1915–16.[64] In another area of the performing arts, Doris Humphrey was a most active and energetic dancer and instructor, renting facilities at the age of nineteen in 1913 to offer lessons. The Scoville Institute, the Nineteenth Century Club, the Oak Park Club and other organizations also continued to sponsor performances of all kinds.

Private social clubs were more respectable places than public ones for the businessmen and merchants to both socialize and enjoy a variety of cultural events. The three largest and earliest clubhouses were all designed by E.E. Roberts. First came the Phoenix Club (one of his designs that clearly shows an early Prairie School influence), opened at Jackson Boulevard and Scoville Avenue in 1902 with a full array of meeting rooms and facilities for billiards, bowling, card playing and other activities, as well as a dining hall, a lounge and a ballroom. A local developer of the area, Allen Flitcraft, rented this facility to the club with an option to apply the monthly fee toward purchase, but the organization failed. Mr. Flitcraft was also the man who later sold the property to the fledgling Ascension Church. The Colonial Club was also designed in 1902, taking its name from its architectural style. Built on Lake Street at Elmwood Avenue, the club contained the same assortment of rooms and activities as its southtown rival but had a somewhat greater family orientation. The last of the three was the Elks Club, designed by Roberts in 1916 and also in a late Prairie Style. Similar in many functions to the other two, it also was built to accommodate the specific fraternal needs of the Elks. Other clubs like the Prairie Cycling Club and the Oak Park Golf Club obviously had ties to specific sports, but neither club ever had the same kind of home as the original three. Only the Golf Club remains, though no longer in an Oak Park location. The Nineteenth Century Club's (by then the Nineteenth Century Woman's Club) final home was built in 1928, and the Oak Park Club completed its major home in 1923. Both substantial buildings still grace the village, though the Oak Park Club ceased operations in 1988.

There was still a lot of open space, south of Madison Street, suitable as a home to the Oak Park Golf Club in the 1890s. The building shown in the photo is assumed to have served as the clubhouse. *Courtesy of HSOPRF.*

The growth and shaping of the community were also being played out in terms of recreation and the availability of open space. While the affluent members of the Golf Club, the cricket players who played at the Old Cricket Grounds and the men who enjoyed the Ridgeland Athletic Bowling Club on Lake Street had places to exercise, few opportunities existed for folks of lesser means and for children to play. State legislation had provided the opportunity for municipalities to create park districts with taxing powers in 1895, but Oak Parkers didn't vote to inaugurate their own district until 1912.

Once elected, the five commissioners quickly set about securing land throughout the village for public parks. Within the first few years, the land for the showpiece park, Scoville Park, was purchased from the Scoville family. The old family mansion was demolished, and landscape architect Jens Jensen was hired to design the space along the Continental Divide. The land earlier used for cricket was also purchased from the Scovilles, and all of the property immediately to its east became Ridgeland Common. South Common (later Rehm Park) serviced the southern portion of the village, and North Park (later Taylor Park), which served the area north of Division Street, was also designed by Jensen in 1914.[65] Over the next three years, additional bits of land adjoining the parks were purchased to enlarge them as those properties became available.

Oliver Wendell Holmes School

Festival Souvenir

Saturday Afternoon, June 6, 1914

In the early years of the twentieth century, school festivals were held every spring. This 1914 brochure from Holmes School listed all of the events and the names of the participants. The day ended with a father and son baseball game. *Courtesy of HSOPRF.*

A village group known as the Small Parks Commission was appointed in 1916, and it was given the charge of recommending sites for playgrounds to the village board. In 1918, utilizing the $90,000 that Oak Park had received as its share of the settlement of the claims regarding the Austin Town Hall land after Austin's annexation—along with the proceeds of a voter-approved bond issue of another $50,000—land was purchased for the creation of five playgrounds. Because of the war, though, nothing was done to purchase equipment for the playgrounds. During this formative period, village, library and park district officials met and planned various joint ventures, including a discussion of sharing resources and a plan for erecting a library in South Park. However, the Illinois Supreme Court ruled such a use of park district land invalid.

On an informal level, much more interaction involving the youth of the community took place in the schools, and many programs that would never be allowed in later times were common aspects of school calendars. Often, daylong Saturday programs were held at the schools, on holidays, at the time of a dedication or anniversary of facilities or at other annual events. On June 6, 1914, for example, Holmes Elementary School celebrated its Annual Play Festival on a Saturday afternoon. Included were dances by students, skits, the Holmes Opera Company performing an operatic melodrama and other performances by both specific classes and clubs. On the athletic side were boxing and wrestling matches, tug of war and a volleyball game between the seventh- and eighth-grade girls. Bringing in the parents, the final event was a baseball game between the eighth-grade boys and their fathers.[66]

All of these plans, proceedings of boards and activities of all of the taxing bodies, the community's organizations and the clubs were reported at length in the major newspapers, as well as in several other short-lived periodicals. However, the *Oak Leaves* became the clear newspaper of record in the first decade of the twentieth century after Henry Austin and some colleagues brokered the merger of the *Oak Park Times* and the *Vindicator* in 1902. The *Oak Leaves* became part of Pioneer Publishing Company in 1915, and a major cast of writers and editors kept it lively and local. Otto McFeely became its longtime editor in 1916, serving and making his views known on all issues until 1950.

Chapter 7

FROM WORLD WAR I TO WORLD WAR II

There had been expansion and progress during the Depression and the war, but many of the public works projects and various appointments were tainted by accusations of political favoritism. As early as 1919, even the Chicago press was noting the ties between Oak Park elected officials and the Republicans of Cicero and Democrats of Chicago. The public was sufficiently aroused that an Oak Park reform slate was elected.[67] Yet the reality of overlapping terms and people elected with different agendas made peace on the board elusive, and charges of corruption continued.

The entry of the United States into World War I in 1917, followed almost immediately by the great influenza epidemic of 1918, slowed the almost frantic pace of development in Oak Park, However, the population continued to grow and reached more than 36,000 by 1918 and almost 40,000 by 1920. The 1930 census shows a number of 63,982. Though the war took young Oak Park lives and influenza claimed many more, the migration into the village from the city and elsewhere was large, with about 15 percent of the population being foreign born by 1930.

The war galvanized local organizations on behalf of our troops, and individuals also did their parts. Most visible were Edgar Rice Burroughs and Ernest Hemingway—the former served as a major in the Illinois Reserves Militia and spoke out to help build morale, and the latter served as a member of the American Red Cross Ambulance Corps in Italy and was wounded several times in the line of duty. Many young Oak Parkers went to war, with 2,446 names of both Oak Parkers and River Forest residents inscribed on

The World War I Peace Monument has graced the hilltop at Scoville Park since 1925. It has undergone a massive restoration and refurbishing, completed in 2010. *Courtesy of Park District of Oak Park.*

the memorial monument in Scoville Park—56 of them had died in service to their country. Interest in the memorial was substantial, with a major funding campaign undertaken between October 15 and October 24, 1921. Contributions and pledges were accepted from 9:00 a.m. through 11:00 p.m. at village hall.[68] The necessary funds were raised, and the monument *Peace Triumphant* was dedicated on November 11, 1925, with Vice President Charles Dawes and General John "Black Jack" Pershing in attendance. No people of color are listed on the memorial, but 9 members of the tiny Mount Carmel Baptist Church were in service during the war, and 1 was killed.[69]

After the war, the various taxing bodies were ready to move on several important and sometimes long-delayed issues, and the village government took the lead on an ambitious program of public works. As automobiles became more and more prevalent and replaced the horse and wagon for both commercial and personal use, the old cedar block form of paving proved totally ineffective, and many streets proved too narrow for cars to navigate. In 1910, Chicago Avenue was the last to replace its blocks with brick paving, and by the early 1920s, asphalt, concrete, brick and macadam were all in use, with asphalt and a concrete mixture the main forms of surfacing both streets and alleys. While some citizens objected to the cost of paving, the widening of Lake and Madison Streets, and Harlem and Oak Park Avenues through the business districts, also meant the removal of many of the old trees planted by the first settlers. That produced a strong negative reaction in the citizenry and a sense that a valuable resource had been lost.

Public transportation was still essential for many villagers, whether to commute to work in Chicago or to get around town if they didn't own a car, but changes were taking place to meet their needs. The County Traction Company, which had taken over all non-Chicago streetcar lines, was known as the West Towns Company after 1913. Many more miles of track had been laid throughout the village and nearby towns, and new lighter trolleys had been purchased. However, by 1922 it had become clear that motorized vehicles were the wave of the future, and both West Towns and Northwestern Transit Company purchased buses and ran lines on all of the arterial and some secondary streets as well.

Starting in 1923, buses connected with the rail lines, with five east–west lines and four running north–south. In 1924, the Northwestern firm became Chicago Rapid Transit Company (now Rapid Transit Authority), running the el. With all of its new buses, West Towns needed a facility to store them, so it built a large garage at Lake Street and Harvey Avenue. West Towns also constantly petitioned the Illinois Commerce Commission to develop new routes and extend old north–south ones as far as North Avenue and south into Berwyn. Some of those routes were never put into operation, and others were discontinued if demand didn't warrant keeping them active. Several reorganizations and mergers occurred throughout the 1930s, but most didn't affect service to an appreciable extent. Citizens complained because West Towns had moved to one-man streetcars, leaving no conductor to control the rowdiness of high school boys.[70] In 1939, in an attempt to increase ridership and in the interest of cooperation with the Chicago Rapid Transit Company, West Towns initiated a bus-trolley transfer system at twenty-five cents. However, the two companies disagreed on the sharing of revenues, and the co-op service was soon dropped.

Three major transportation issues kept the interest and attention of the citizens, the various commissions and the press. One issue concerned the possible elimination of all streetcars, as many felt that they created both safety and noise issues; another was the possibility of consolidating all trolley lines under the authority of the Chicago City Council, with no voice given to the suburban communities that they served; the third was elevating the rail lines. The first issue took care of itself as fixed trolley lines became less viable; the second control issue continued beyond the time buses replaced the electric cars, ending with the reorganization of West Towns after the firm's declaring bankruptcy in 1937, when a major fire at the car barn destroyed twenty-five streetcars. The firm borrowed cars from the Chicago Surface line, but citizens felt them to be too noisy and unsafe. To make things worse, a 1940 accident knocked out some lines at a time when the lack of gas for cars was increasing the need for electric transit. With the increased ridership, the West Towns Company reorganized and reconstructed the lines, but the firm went bankrupt again in 1942. Raising the railroad tracks when they entered Oak Park was an ongoing issue for decades, starting with community expressions of concern about the frequency of accidents and the traffic delays caused by having to stop driving at so many intersections when trains were going by. A remedial plan was accepted by the village board in January 1907, but nothing came of it. After the railroad was placed in the hands of a receiver in 1911, no further steps were taken until 1921. At that time, with bonds in hand, there was another push to elevate the tracks. But this time the property owners along South Boulevard were able to get the courts to stop the plan on the grounds that the proposed embankment would leave the street too narrow for vehicular traffic.[71] There were additional proposals and suggested solutions offered in the years ahead, but the trains remained on grade for decades.

Without any public opposition to having sufficient water of the greatest purity, the Cicero Township and then the village governments had constantly added newer and deeper wells and increased the number and capacity of water mains. The village had taken over the water distribution system in 1912, but there remained a fear that the City of Chicago could not or would not satisfy local needs when the demand was highest. So, at a special election in August 1924, the voters of Oak Park were asked to approve the issuance of bonds to support the construction of an underground reservoir of reinforced concrete with a capacity of 5 million gallons. The proposal was approved, and the facility was placed just east of the village's pumping station, underneath playgrounds and playing fields.[72]

The new piping installed at that time originated at the pumping station, immediately increasing availability and better water pressure. With minor changes, the water system and the relationship with Chicago as supplier

The 5-million-gallon reservoir was opened in the mid-1920s, and five of the village trustees visited on an inspection tour in the 1940s. Dorothy Kerr was the first female trustee and was continuously elected from 1927 to 1945. *Courtesy of HSOPRF.*

remain in force today. Drainage was a more complicated issue, however, producing constant concern about the water table, flooding of basements and, sometimes, the impassability of the streets after heavy rainfalls. The latitudinal streets along the core were reasonably well serviced, but the newer areas to the north and south were not protected, so various corrective steps were taken. First, in 1923, the village arranged to divert the sewage from the main area to the lines of the sanitary district and then saw the pressure on the north end relieved when the district constructed another sewer to drain that area. Later in the 1920s and through the mid-1930s, the village worked with the sanitary district and other nearby municipalities, going so far as to set up a Drainage Relief Committee to get federal support that finally resulted in major work in 1935 and 1936 and the connection of the new Oak Park facilities with those of the Chicago Sanitary District. Thus, with the population approaching its high of about seventy-two thousand, the village had the capacity needed for appropriate sanitation.

A new village-wide system was installed in 1927, after the proposal to provide lights for every street in town survived litigation and being the major issue in a municipal election that spring. More than four thousand lights replaced the antiquated fixtures and were installed over the summer and

The first field houses were completed in the 1920s and named after writers and poets. This photo shows children engaged in nature study at Eugene Field Playground Center. *Courtesy of Park District of Oak Park.*

fall, and the job of replacing all of the poles and wires was completed ahead of schedule, at a cost of more than $1 million for the plant and the light fixtures. The village board boasted that Oak Park was now "the best lighted community in the world."[73] Garbage was disposed of in a variety of ways, with the village operating an incinerator plant at North Boulevard and East Avenue. The plant burned somewhere between fifty and seventy-five tons of garbage daily, much of it generated by local businesses favoring that method over landfill disposal, as the village didn't charge them for the use of the incinerator service.

At the end of the war, the community had the luxury of returning to the subject of recreation, acquiring the rest of the land necessary for the creation of playgrounds and allocating the funds for the equipment to be used by children. First, some $20,000 was provided to equip two of the playgrounds. Then, the additional funds needed were raised through the levy of a special tax for playgrounds permitted by the state and approved by the voters in April 1921. The village trustees made their commission into an official playground board, and the first four playgrounds were opened that summer. Some centers just contained swing sets, climbing apparatus and other standard equipment, and others also contained tennis courts.

A major innovation, later touted as the first in the United States, was the construction of the field houses as the result of a design competition won by local Prairie School architect John van Bergen. A staff was hired, and various citizen groups worked on the programming at each center. A couple of years later, as another innovative gesture, each playground was given the name of a famous author of children's literature: Hans Christian Anderson, Lewis Carroll, Eugene Field, Henry Wadsworth Longfellow and Robert Louis Stevenson. The field houses were finished in 1928, and they became the centers of dramatics, storytelling for young children and other expanded programming. There were art projects associated with the centers, too, and paintings were installed representing major scenes from the writings of each author after whom a center was named.

When, as so often happened, citizens expressed concern about the potential rowdiness of youth, the playground board approved the creation of a volunteer junior police force to make sure that the playground equipment was used properly. The volunteers' duties included enforcing order on the grounds, running errands and serving as ushers at major playground events. By 1930, roughly 500,000 visits to the centers were made annually, with extravaganzas like water performances drawing large crowds. In the same decade, there was also major growth of large parks, with Maple and Fox Parks opening in 1921 and 1922, respectively. Also at this time, many members of the park board began to serve for long periods of time, being reelected for periods of up to twenty years. This differed from the village board, for which a few terms were usually the norm.

In addition to the mural projects for the field houses and the art courses taught there, a number of painters, the sculptor Richard Bock and the architect Charles White had formed a broad-based Fine Arts Society in 1908; it held annual exhibitions at the Scoville Institute and elsewhere. Carl Krafft was one of the most successful artists, with a Chicago reputation. He got together some of the other Oak Park artists to meet and discuss art at his home in 1919. They officially started the Oak Park Art League in 1921, renting and borrowing space for their exhibitions, often at the Wright Studio nearby and in Chicago. Later, although the Great Depression placed most cultural organizations at a standstill or caused them to fold, the art league did intensive fundraising and bought the 1901 E.E. Roberts–designed stable and coach house on Chicago Avenue in 1937, a building that Doris Humphrey had previously rented to offer dance lessons. The number of well-known artists who either lived in Oak Park or chose to at least affiliate with the art league was impressive. The almost two hundred dues-paying

SOMETHING GOING ON
AT THE ART LEAGUE

Saturday Night, November 7

Henry g. F o o t e   Anna til den
Carl r. KrafFt   maud WilSON
Frederick gerlach   Cornelia wey burn   Laura HaLes

Of Course There Will Be GRo CERiES
and Music [Such as it is]

carl R. KRAFFT exhibition on view.

Above: Before the Ridgeland and Rehm swimming pools were opened in the 1960s, the shallow pool at Stevenson Center was the site of pageants, performances and water sports. *Courtesy of Park District of Oak Park.*

Left: The Oak Park Art League was founded in 1921 and held its exhibitions and classes at several locations, until it purchased its Chicago Avenue home in 1937. Carl Krafft, the league's founder, taught not only locally but also at the art institute. *Courtesy of Oak Park Art League.*

regular members included Loredo Taft, Raymond Shiva, Pauline Palmer, Walter Ufer, Carl Hoeckner and Karl Buehr.[74]

Music continued to have a greater presence in the village, with many of the earlier organizations replaced by the Civic Music Association of Oak Park, formed in 1924. It became the main vehicle for bringing well-known musical performers and groups to the community, the Warrington Opera House, the library and other institutions. After the opening of both the Oak Park Club's new headquarters in 1923 and the Nineteenth Century Woman's Club's new building in 1928, two major venues were added for both concerts and lectures on the arts.

Among the organizations that performed at both at one time or another was the Symphony of Oak Park and River Forest, one of the earliest community orchestras in the United States. It had its origins as a Sunday school orchestra at a Presbyterian church and was organized in 1931 by its first and longtime conductor, Gladys Welge, a child prodigy who had already directed her family's music school at the age of seventeen. She concurrently served as principal conductor of the Chicago Women's Orchestra for several years. The local group often brought in Metropolitan Opera singers, Chicago Symphony Orchestra members and local choruses to join them in performances. In founding the Symphony of Oak Park and River Forest, which she led for twenty-three years, Welge followed in the footsteps of Grace Hemingway and her Oak Park Choral Society and Mrs. Palmer Hulbert and her Rubinstein Club, both of whom had leadership roles in directing excellent musical organizations.

While such leadership by women was not unknown elsewhere, that women founded and/or led three of the major musical organizations clearly indicates leadership rather than passive patronage in Oak Park. But an even greater indication of the growing roles of women in the community was the election of the first female trustee, Dorothy C. Kerr, in 1927, as well as her service on the board for eighteen consecutive years. After graduating from Vassar, Kerr had worked as a children's librarian in the Oak Park Library and served on almost every board in the community. An omnivorous participant in Oak Park causes and local organizations, Kerr was the president of the Day Nursery and the Nineteenth Century Club and a member on other boards. After retiring from the Oak Park Village Board in 1943, she was appointed village auditor and served in that role for two years. In the range of her activities, she rivaled men like James Scoville.

Another area of leadership by women was their continuous string of service as the village's innovative head librarians. The library board had taken over the entire Scoville Institute building by the mid-1910s, and a

The Nineteenth Century Club was founded in 1891. Its members have always participated in social, charitable and educational activities, holding leadership positions in many organizations and on elected boards. The building was opened in 1928 and still offers weekly programs for its members and their guests. *Courtesy of the author.*

deposit station for circulating library books had opened in a drugstore on Chicago Avenue. This facility proved so popular that a branch library was sited a few blocks east in 1923, balancing out the earlier rented facility known as the South Branch at Harrison Street. Under the energetic leadership of Elsie McKay, a branch was established on South Oak Park Avenue in 1928, but it became a casualty of the Great Depression in 1932.

In another great tribute to the commitment to culture and education of Oak Parkers of that era, voters approved a bond issue in 1935, enabling the library board to purchase a site on Harrison at Gunderson. A grant was obtained from the Public Works Administration of the federal government, and E.E. Roberts and his son designed the permanent structure, later named Maze after its longtime librarian.[75] Yet with all the support of culture, the community had a board of censorship in the 1930s, with its primary attention directed at theater and movies, leaving it to the library staff and board to censor reading matter. Live theater had pretty well given way to the movies in the 1930s in Oak Park, and a large new movie house, the Lake Theater, opened in 1936. A classic example of Art Deco theater style, with 1,420 seats

The branch library on Gunderson Avenue was designed by E.E. Roberts and his son, Elmer Roberts, in a Georgian architectural style. It was opened in 1936 and was renamed in honor of its longtime librarian, Adele Maze, upon her death in 1957. *Courtesy of the author.*

in the one hall, the Lake grew and changed much later on, adapting to the times but maintaining the look of its origins.

Both cultural awareness and a sense of being a special community seem to have been part of the development of Oak Park since its earliest days. In addition to all of the organizations, groups and institutions already mentioned, various pioneers wrote about themselves and the community as early as 1898, when there was an abortive attempt to organize a historical society. Other attempts were made, including the appointment of a committee by the village president, with the mission of collecting material related to Oak Park's local history and to have the material preserved and available at the library. Teachers from the local schools and the junior college, as well as longtime citizens, were asked to serve. At the second meeting, the list of names of those at the 1898 meeting was presented by the son of one of the participants.[76] But this group never reached maturity, either, and disappeared. Many years later, in February 1937, another ad hoc group met at the South Branch of the library and organized the Historical Society of Oak Park. The branch librarian became the historian and

Fenwick High School was opened in the fall of 1929 as a Roman Catholic college preparatory institution for boys. The school admitted young women in 1992 and offers a rigorous academic program. *Courtesy of Fenwick High School.*

keeper of records, a group of officers was elected and dues were set for the purpose of supporting the organization.

Four public elementary schools were established after the village became independent: Lincoln in 1906, Irving in 1910, Hatch in 1922 and Mann in 1927, though almost all of the original group were either rebuilt or added to one or more times throughout the 1930s, as the school population more than kept pace with the population at large. Thus the district had eleven elementary schools and an administrative wing. In 1930, the enrollment was more than five thousand pupils. The high school was also enlarged through the years, with a wing for manual training added in 1912, an east wing in 1919–21 and the west wing and cafeteria in 1924–25. The field house was reported to be the first in the nation when constructed in 1927, and a stadium was completed and dedicated in 1924.[77] By 1930, the high school housed almost four thousand students and was also attracting a number of fee-paying out-of-district pupils. The first known public nursery school, called the Community Pre-Kindergarten School, opened in the fall of 1929, with about fifty children enrolled.

There were parochial schools at all four Roman Catholic churches in Oak Park by the late 1920s, as well as Christ Evangelical Lutheran School. In addition, a Roman Catholic precollege military academy was founded in 1917. Named Bishop Quarter School, after a Chicago prelate, it differed from the other Catholic institutions in that it took both day and boarding pupils, and its curriculum was both rigorous and traditional. Fenwick High School was opened in the fall of 1929 as a boys-only college preparatory facility and the first Dominican-run institution west of the Allegheny Mountains. By the beginning of the 1930s, all of the pre–World War II educational institutions and their major additions and annexes were in place, and an important, but short-lived, junior college had been founded.

For some years, there had been talk of a local two-year college to provide the basics of the liberal arts curriculum and prepare people to transfer to four-year institutions. Although the high school board was very much in favor of supporting the venture, no funds were available to acquire appropriate space at first. But the closing of North (formerly Sixth) Congregational Church, when the congregation was absorbed into that of Pilgrim, provided an opportunity for the planned junior college to move into the community house that had been constructed by North Church in 1926.

The building was almost new but ill-suited to the diverse needs of a college, so Oak Park and River Forest High School rented its laboratories for science classes, and the Oak Park Library provided many services. The junior college opened in 1933 with five full-time employees: president, registrar, dean, librarian and office manager, as well as nine part-time instructors and thirty-five students. When the college closed, a victim of the Depression, it had seventeen faculty members and

In the early 1930s, citizens felt that a low-cost but high-quality education could be obtained by founding a junior college with a curriculum oriented toward transfer to universities. The college didn't survive the Great Depression, and the village leases space for the Dole Branch Library. Postcard. *Courtesy of the author.*

ninety-nine students, with half of the students transferring to such substantial institutions as the University of Chicago, University of Illinois, Northwestern University and many other private and public universities. In view of the already solid reputation of the high school, each of those universities accepted all credits from the junior college without examination. Tuition was low, but even with the support of the community, the junior college couldn't survive and pay its modest bills, closing after five years in 1938.

When the college was closed, according to a piece in the *Review*, a pamphlet published in conjunction with the fiftieth anniversary of its closing and reunion, "There had been rumors that some undesirable organization was trying to buy the property, and by 1939 Arthur Dole had bought it; in 1940 it was officially given to the Village of Oak Park."[78] There is no incriminating written evidence of the type noted in regard to prejudice against the opening of either Mount Zion or Ascension Church, but it has long been understood that the "undesirable organization" that wished to purchase the building for its use was a synagogue. As there was clear and specific opposition when Jewish congregations tried to build synagogues at later dates, the assumption that they were not wanted in 1939 seems quite reasonable.

During the 1920s and the slowdown during the Depression, several large churches replaced smaller ones for their growing congregations, especially those of the Baptists, who opened both First Baptist in 1923 and Judson Baptist, which was started in 1922 and completed in 1930. Presbyterian congregations grew and merged, as did those of the Lutherans, with United Evangelical Lutheran on North Ridgeland Avenue being the result of the merger of three area churches in 1928. Two of the Methodist congregations built new churches in the 1920s. After that, there was a slow but steady shift of membership from the older congregations to newer ones, with consolidation and some closings.

Highlighting the parallel existence of the very formal and traditional large congregations of most of the major Protestant denominations and the growing Catholic churches was the increase in churches not affiliated with any one denomination. While two had earlier roots, most of them grew in the 1920s and erected their buildings in that period. Similarly, the Baha'i of Oak Park and the Theosophical Society were growing into mature organizations at that time. However, as neither had its own buildings nor paid clergy, details about the extent of their membership are not clear.

In the early years after the First World War, the continued boom in population was matched by the increase in the number of apartment houses being built and attempts to regulate growth in a variety of ways. As already noted, the community was hostile to the development of multiunit buildings, as evidenced when the first two flats and residential hotels had been built, and a 1902 ordinance had stipulated that buildings of three or more apartments had to be constructed of brick, iron, stone or some other fireproof material. Various other restrictions were instituted at that time, and others were added through the years thereafter. Most of the apartment hotels, including the largest, the Oak Park Arms, were built on major arterial streets and had less impact on the residents of single-family houses than they might have had otherwise. In addition, particularly along Austin and Washington Boulevards, where many apartment houses were developed, "[a]rchitects and builders made obvious attempts to incorporate features usually reserved for the construction of single-family houses: tile roofs, casement windows, art glass and a variety of exterior ornament."[79]

Developers went so far as to break up the mass of the buildings by developing many around courtyards and including porches and sunrooms to soften the façades. However, those steps were insufficient to suit those who most worried about the loss of the feeling of suburbia that the inclusion of larger apartment houses might create. Arguments were either directed

The Oak Park Arms is the oldest surviving residential hotel in Oak Park. Opened in 1921 with parking, a salon, retail stores and a restaurant, there were additions in 1927 and 1928. Now a senior citizen residence, it still boasts amenities and services, including entertainment. *Courtesy of the author.*

to that point or stressed fear of such problems as disease and crime as the reasons to exclude them. Typical of the many letters and articles in the press was an editorial from 1913 stressing that a proposed ordinance regulating flats didn't go far enough with regard to sanitation: "It still would permit of air and vent shafts with windows opening upon them from pantries, and bath rooms and water closets. This is a relic of barbarism that belongs in the same class with the old-fashioned country outhouse."[80]

Fear of an onslaught of large lot line to lot line apartment buildings prompted the village to pass its first zoning ordinance in 1921, the second such ordinance in Illinois, primarily as a tool to regulate the kinds of buildings erected, especially in residential neighborhoods. An application had been submitted for a proposed fifty-two-unit apartment building at Pleasant Street and Euclid Avenue, an area composed of single-family homes. After the residents complained, the village refused to grant a building permit. Then the new zoning board, of which a highly respected architect, Charles White, was the first chair, called a meeting, zoning that area as had been proposed some months earlier. The new zoning ordinance had not taken effect while the state legislature was reviewing it, and the developers held that they were not subject to the new rules. Judge Morrell decided in favor of the village and its police power, noting that "the rights of property had been 'shot to pieces' during the war and afterward, especially by the decision of the United States Supreme Court in the decision legalizing the rent commission and laws changing the traditional relation of landlord and tenant."[81] Some months later, the Illinois Supreme Court upheld the constitutionality of zoning and laws to define it.

Real estate firms and property developers objected to the zoning and the limits it placed on their ability to do what they wanted with their properties. They complained that the law was the equivalent of confiscation and that flat living was now vital for people who once would have lived in large houses. They felt that only the most expensive buildings would be permitted under the new regulations.

That there was some truth to their point can be seen in the ads for the development of some of the grander apartment complexes of the day, appealing both to the quality of the buildings and enticing local investors to buy the bonds with which the developers were financing the buildings. A prospectus for the Santa Maria Apartments offered bonds from $100 to $10,000, at an interest rate of 7 percent, and made lavish claims for the location and amenities in the three-, four- and five-room units. The battle for and against apartment developments continued throughout the decade, while testimony at public hearings and letters to the editor give personal accounts of the loss of profit incurred by those who could not see their properties developed into large hotels or apartment houses because of the zoning ordinance and the readiness of neighbors to object to anything large in their neighborhood. In a letter to the editor in 1927, Bevanee Marshal Matlack complained about her inability to use property her husband gave her, referring to the "arbitrary power of the zoning board." The next sentence threw in an anti-Semitic reference when she mentions "sing [*sic*] the Jewish lullaby, buy low, sell high."[82] In spite of the opposition, the zoning ordinances remained in force, though they were amended many times and were a powerful tool in both regulating and encouraging development.

The village board got far less negative feedback when it investigated and moved to control rooming houses. The real estate developers who wished to build apartment houses had no interest in seeing squalid rooming houses in the vicinity of their buildings and possibly saw renters moving into their smaller apartments if the rooming houses were closed. Matters came to a head in early 1940, when the physician who served as the health commissioner joined

Between the end of the Great Depression and the early 1960s, Lake Street between Forest and Harlem Avenues was the center of commercial activity, from Woolworth's and Marshall Field's. This photo shows Lake Street looking west from Marion Street. *Courtesy of Downtown Oak Park.*

with the fire chief to outline the results of their investigation of such dwellings. They found more than one hundred rooming houses in the village, with some owners owning several and some having as many as twenty-five people in one building. The conditions in some of the buildings were described as deplorable, prompting the health commissioner to recommend regulation of these dwellings, as they were violating health, zoning and fire regulations. The village board unanimously voted to control these residences in March 1940.[83]

Residential growth was more than matched by the growth and expansion of business beyond that of additional groceries, cleaners, teashops and clothing stores. Major department stores began moving into the village starting in 1923, when the Hub (later Lytton's) opened an Oak Park branch. The Fair (later Montgomery Ward) and Marshall Field's opened in 1929, and Hillman's, Baskins, Bramson's, Peck and Peck and others soon followed. That growth and the concentration of all of those stores solidified the village's reputation as a shopping center for the western suburbs and many to the south as well. This was especially true with regard to the Marshall Field's building, not only the largest of the department stores but also located at the prominent intersection of Lake and Harlem, while enjoying the prestige and reputation as Chicago's premier retail company. The stores in Oak Park and Evanston, which were almost identical in appearance, opened at about the same time in 1929. (Incidentally, and as an indication of the changing face of merchandising, they both closed on the same day in 1986.)

Adding to the retail mix, most major automobile dealers had showrooms in Oak Park by the outbreak of World War II, with the majority of them located on Madison Street. The presence of various other auto-related businesses, such as suppliers and repair facilities, made the village "Automobile Row" for the western suburbs. New businesses opened on Oak Park Avenue, south of Van Buren Street, and as a result of the growth of both business and residential demand, a southside post office opened in rented space around 1925, replacing the one near Harlem.

The businessmen as a group responded to all of this growth with a new spirit of cooperation and community. For example, they formed an Association of the Central Business District and advertised heavily in the local press. Their message was clear: "An aggressive campaign to prove to the customer that he gains by spending his money at home will be launched to hold the Christmas trade in Oak Park."[84] Soon, a South Oak Park Commercial Association was also actively promoting its business district.

A byproduct of all this growth—accompanied by the increase in the population from just under forty thousand in 1920 to more than sixty thousand in 1930—was the dislocation of both people and smaller businesses from the main shopping districts. Not only couldn't the small businesses necessarily compete for the shopper's dollar, but they also couldn't usually afford the rents that the chains were willing to pay for prime retail space. And as the much larger footprint of the department stores meant that there were fewer individuals with whom to negotiate leases, the building owners were happy to work with chain management.

Another aspect of dislocation was the effective removal of residential units and enclaves in the busiest commercial areas. This trend hit the African American community the hardest, especially as the small community was concentrated around the church on William Street. When developers wished to expand onto that block, both residents and black-owned businesses were swept away. Mount Carmel Church, already hit with a fire that may well have been set, was sold by the congregation, and the members scattered to Maywood, Chicago and Judson Baptist Church in east Oak Park.[85] A series of handsome new English Tudor buildings opened in the renamed Westgate, but the heart of the African American community had been removed. Some black individuals and families who lived in other parts of town remained, but their numbers and their few remaining businesses dwindled over the next few decades.

The Oak Park Conservatory's greenhouses were opened in 1929 and always provided winter opportunities to enjoy nature. A citizen's group rallied to save it in 1970, and an all-purpose addition opened in 2000. *Courtesy of the author.*

Though the center of commerce was along Lake Street, at Harlem and Oak Park Avenues, and all of the major public buildings were in and along Lake Street as well, the park board took advantage of buying an unused factory building on Garfield Street, at a very reasonable price, near the middle of the village for use as its headquarters in 1928. The new conservatory was erected nearby in 1929, providing an indoor venue for the enjoyment of nature in the long winter season when outdoor plantings were dormant. In an increasingly rare example of intergovernmental cooperation, the village conveyed the vacant land where the former "dummy" railroad stations had stood along Randolph Street to the park district for use as miniature parks, while the park district also beautified the parkway strips along the Kenilworth and LeMoyne Parkways. Bits and pieces of land continued to be acquired and added to many of the parks, increasing both their size and range of utility. With the passing of the last of the private athletic clubs in this era, the parks became the centers for sport and recreation for most of the public, except for those affluent enough to join the Oak Park Country Club or one of the private tennis clubs.

The main post office in Oak Park was designed in a late Art Deco style by Charles White and was constructed between 1933 and 1936. J. Theodore Johnson painted the four murals depicting Illinois history, but the public was unhappy that a local artist wasn't given the commission. *Courtesy of the author.*

During the Depression, the only major piece of construction that was built that had not been funded and initiated earlier was a major new post office for the village, a building designed by Charles White, who was already known for the eclectic architectural styles that he had embraced and utilized since leaving Wright's studio while Unity Temple was under construction. Mentioned earlier as the first chair of the Zoning Commission of Oak Park, White had designed a variety of local buildings. Three homes were demolished to provide space for the new building after White had submitted plans in 1932 for his late Art Deco–style structure. The plans were officially approved, and the building, which was both modern in style and incorporated the latest technology, was constructed between 1933 and 1936; it immediately become a source of local pride. Murals inside the building were a creation of 1938, under the Section of Painting and Sculpture of the Treasury Art Project, and created controversy because no local artists had been considered. Other local federal relief projects were mainly concerned with more basic infrastructure.

Of course, some businesses failed in Oak Park, as elsewhere, and there was fear that local banks and savings and loans might fail. Examiners from the state auditor's office and the Federal Reserve visited both Oak Park Trust and Savings Bank and Suburban Trust and Savings Bank in March 1933, and the two of them, as well as Avenue and Prairie State Bank, remained open.[86] Oak Park Trust was so pressed for capital, though, that Henry Austin sold his Lake Street frontage and moved his home back on his property to raise funds to keep the bank open.

The national economy was in shambles with the deepening of the Depression, but the situation in Oak Park was complicated by two issues relating to taxation. First of all, the state was very slow in getting monies paid to the village that were promised and due. In February 1930, an appeal was sent to Governor Louis L. Emmerson requesting that overdue funds be paid so that bankruptcy could be avoided. "Surely no well regulated business organization would be allowed to flounder along without collecting its accounts receivable" was the thrust of the argument and served as part of an appeal for at least temporary legislation to support the release of funds.[87] Village president Charles Crysler also asked Evanston, River Forest, Berwyn and Forest Park to join in the appeal, but it isn't clear if they ever did so. The other problem facing Oak Park was more specifically in regard to the assessed evaluation of property in the collar suburbs versus that in Chicago. The local press, at the same time that it was reporting on the problem of obtaining funds due from the state, noted that the evaluations for similar properties in Chicago were assessed at no greater than one-third of the amount assessed in Oak Park and River Forest.[88] All involved in Oak Park and River Forest were convinced that the county officials were consciously discriminating against the suburbs in favor of Chicago's large body of voters.

A scandal occurred at the same time that Oak Park was facing all of those fiscal issues. The village had an elected officer, the police magistrate, who served as a judge, hearing cases brought against individuals who violated local ordinances. The magistrate, rather than receiving a salary, was entitled to keep the court costs, thus having an incentive to find "against" plaintiffs. Though the Illinois legislature had granted home rule communities the right to replace that system with their own municipal courts, Oak Park had not done so until James M. Faron, the magistrate, disappeared in November 1929 and was found to have embezzled more than $15,000. When he was captured in March 1930, the village board quickly abolished the office of magistrate, allowing for a salaried elected judge to hear local cases.

During the midst of the Depression, and with all the issues facing individuals, families and the community, there were still reasons to celebrate the growth of the village. A celebration of the 100th anniversary

Decorated floats were a part of many parades through most of the twentieth century. This float celebrates the centennial of the settlement of Oak Park and may have been part of the celebrations at the Century of Progress Fair. *Courtesy of Park District of Oak Park.*

of Kettlestrings's settlement in what was to become Oak Park was held at several venues at the Century of Progress World's Fair in 1933. An Oak Park Day was organized, with the Oak Park Art League mounting an exhibit at the Horticultural Building, with music provided by various school bands and with children's programs that grew out of the playground and field house staff efforts. A local author, Zoe Mae Hakes, wrote and scripted a major revue that traced the development of the village from the movement along the Indian trails to that time, with vignettes relating to the early settlers and such events as the Civil War and the separation from Cicero Township. As noted in reference to the support of the community for the library bond issue, the creation of the historical society and the growth of the parks during the Depression, this celebration also demonstrated that a substantial majority of its citizenry believed that Oak Park was indeed a village worth celebrating.

At a more basic level of survival, practical steps were taken to respond to the situation that people faced. Throughout the Great Depression, the parks, the conservatory and the field houses continued to be centers of activity and recreation. Those opportunities were enhanced by the 1939 purchase of the Mills estate, formerly owned by the flamboyant and philanthropic John Farson. With a large mansion available to house activities, and with substantial open land in a part of town short of such space, the park district found another opportunity to expand horizons and provide recreational resources for the community. Yet many of the programs offered by the district were also oriented to helping with skill development, aimed at making people employable. So, as the result of state legislation that permitted the township to make a levy for "Poor Relief," the township government placed on the township supervisor the responsibility for aiding impoverished citizens. Poor Relief, later known as General Assistance to distinguish it from any specific federal programs, was the first of the township's responses to social needs and set a new reason for distinguishing this support from the more concrete services provided by the village government. To enable effective utilization of the resources, a professional social worker was added to the township staff.

The entry of the United States into World War II and the shift to a wartime economy initiated many changes in the way people conducted their lives, spent their leisure time and utilized transportation options. However, there were very few changes to the way any of the branches of local government operated.

Chapter 8

POSTWAR CHALLENGES

The most important and immediate problem faced at the end of World War II was a need for housing for returning veterans and their families. As many had married during the war and deferred finding their own apartments or homes, the pent-up demand for housing was impossible to meet with the existing units in Oak Park and elsewhere. Housing was in such short supply that the Oak Park–River Forest High School publicly aired the idea that it might have to stop hiring married male teachers because they couldn't find homes in the area. The village board felt the need to respond to two aspects of the shortage: the practices of unscrupulous landlords and the need to actually create new housing.

The first concern had two parts. One was the reality that some building owners were using the housing shortage as an excuse to raise rents to whatever levels they felt they could. Second, and even more emotionally laden, was the concern over evicting people who were behind on their rent or to free up their apartment for someone who would pay more. In response, the board passed an ordinance in July 1946 limiting residential property rent increases to 10 percent of the maximum rent provided by the Office of Price Administration rent control regulations then recently promulgated, to prevent any possible rent gouging. Further, the board passed a unanimous resolution directing the police department to prevent landlords from evicting tenants without due process of law.[89]

To deal with the housing shortage itself, the village government created the Oak Park Housing Authority in 1946, with the express mission of providing housing for returning veterans. After the state government allocated

With housing demand for returning World War II veterans impossible to meet, the newly established Housing Authority built groups of the same kind of Quonset huts that had been used for temporary housing during the war. Small but fully equipped, they served as stopgap housing and were demolished in the early 1950s. *Courtesy of Donna King.*

110 units of housing to Oak Park, the search was on to find the space to develop the units quickly. Heartwarming stories in the local press told of local families and businesses offering to donate their own land to enable the development of housing for these families, but the plots were often too small to be of use. More important, strategically, the Housing Authority felt that it would be more efficient if the units were grouped together rather than on scattered lots.[90] Working with the park district, the village and the Housing Authority assembled the land and overcame the "not in my backyard" initial responses of many of the neighbors in the areas designated for the housing. The veterans and their families were organized and respectful and hit the soft spot of some of the opponents' hearts, winning them over. Few, after all, would deny a place to live to a veteran who had been wounded or worse.

The plan was approved, utilizing the $84,000 in allocated state funds, and seventy-six prefabricated Quonset huts were erected within months. The temporary units were twenty by fifty-four feet and contained two bedrooms, a living room, a combined kitchen and dining area and a bathroom. All had standard utilities of water, electricity and gas in addition to oil-heated furnaces. Demand exceeded supply, so other families had to live with relatives or look elsewhere for housing. Yet with the resumption of new construction as soon as materials became available, many new homes and apartment houses were built in both Oak Park and neighboring communities. As early as the end of 1948, the Housing Authority took the first step toward providing more permanent housing and built a four-unit apartment structure on one of the sites. The Quonset huts had served their purpose by 1952 and were all demolished by the end of 1953.

A temporary and minor test of the community's ability to promote cooperation among all the taxing bodies and the citizenry came in the winter of 1950, during a national coal miners' strike. As much of the local electricity was generated by coal-burning plants, the authorities called for a voluntary 25 percent cut of electric usage, to diminish the impact and frequency of brownouts. The two hospitals felt a greater impact than other services, and most people dug in for the short duration. The only ones sorry to have the strike ended were the schoolchildren who were enjoying the cut in their schedules and the early dismissal of classes.

Public transportation again became a big issue after the war as the automotive industry shifted from war production to building family cars. Once again, the West Towns Company was reorganized after its second bankruptcy, and its new president increased the rate of conversion from electric trolleys to buses. Electric trolleys held on into the 1950s, but automobile-owning citizens were demanding more lanes for cars, and the trolley's days were numbered. West Towns had about three hundred on staff, most of whom ran the system that eventually totaled 125 buses in fourteen west suburban routes from the Oak Park headquarters. Yet with the growth of car ownership, the company struggled to remain competitive and relevant to the community. At the same time, other transportation options were opening: others had tried to develop taxi service, and Blue Cab began operating in 1923. In 1946, the company started intravillage service with a fare of seven cents, creating options with which fixed lines and buses and their infrequently scheduled runs found it hard to compete.

The Chicago Transit Company's trains had long been the major source of transportation to and from downtown Chicago, but certain issues lingered after the war. The number of stations and the time taken to stop at each one were a source of frustration for years. One approach to providing speedier service was the establishment of A and B stations in 1948. At the same time, several infrequently used stations in proximity to others were closed. When decisions were being made as to which ones to close or consolidate, influential Oak Parkers lobbied to keep all of the Oak Park stations open and on both the A and B lines, serving the village. Similar pressure with regard to downtown service was applied in later years. Less easily handled was the dangerous nature of the

Lake Street El running at grade through Oak Park, as accidents had persisted ever since the line's inception. Of the twenty-two grade-level crossings between Laramie and Harlem stations, fourteen were in Oak Park. Finally, in the first known instance of diesel and electrified trains sharing the same embankment, the Northwestern Railroad and what earlier had become the Chicago Transit Authority agreed to raise the tracks to the embankment, putting an end to a situation that both was dangerous and created a lot of backed-up traffic.

By far the biggest transportation issue of the era was the plan to build what eventually became the Eisenhower Expressway. The topic had been broached in the context of a series of superhighways as early as 1939, with a few more details mentioned the following year. That the expressway would be a below-street-level road, built along the path of both the Baltimore and Ohio Railroad and the then Congress Elevated, was a given, though the early assumption was also made that it would be a toll road. A model was actually presented to a meeting of the local chamber of commerce in 1941, but the wartime reality was that no such road was going to be built with so many able-bodied men at war or supporting the war effort in their work as civilians. Toward the end of World War II, as talk of the highway was initiated by the U.S. Department of Highways, there were mixed reactions to the details of the proposal.

Most Oak Parkers and other residents of the western suburbs were generally favorable toward the project, with the local feeling being that the highway would both cut commuting time and create more demand for housing in what would be an even more convenient Oak Park; there was also the feeling that the project would cut traffic generated by suburbanites who drove through the village on their way downtown. Also significant was the probability that accidents involving pedestrians or cars would virtually be eliminated by having depressed train tracks with overpasses instead of crossings at ground level. Yet there were three major issues of concern: the location of the tracks, both the railroad and the CTA; the number and location of overpasses and ramps; and the loss of homes and businesses in the path of and abutting the highway. Especially vexing to the village board was the projected loss of up to seventy-four single-family homes and thirty-seven apartment units, as well as the probability of having to replace the fire station on Garfield Street, which would be in the footprint of the road.[91] The number of displacements was modest, extending over the almost two miles of the highway in Oak Park. The railroad and CTA trains were already there, and there were no streets between Harrison and Garfield. But the issues had to be addressed, and were, over the next few years as plans were refined through negotiations during the early years of the 1950s.

The construction of the Eisenhower Expressway was started in 1955 and completed in 1960. The Oak Park section was built at a cost of $10 million. *Courtesy of HSOPRF.*

The issue of the location and number of entrance/exit ramps was very contentious, as the original plan was to have three: at Austin Boulevard, East Avenue and Harlem Avenue. When the citizens, the staff of the churches and schools along East Avenue and the village demurred, the county suggested Ridgeland Avenue as an alternative. Eventually, in the fall of 1955, ten thousand people signed a petition to Governor William Stratton, opposing a ramp at either location, and the county backed off.[92] The citizens also pushed for more overpasses, but a compromise left a footbridge over Home Avenue and the inclusion of overpasses at Austin Boulevard, East Avenue, Ridgeland Avenue, Oak Park Avenue and Harlem Avenue, adding an additional one at Lombard Avenue, with the state paying for all of them.

The most difficult issue to resolve, and one that the village totally lost, was in regard to the placement of the tracks. The county and the railroad wanted the tracks on the south side, and the village and CTA wanted the railroad down the center. However, the B&O Railroad and local businesses that wanted access to the railroad for shipping proved to be more powerful, at the state level, creating the need for the destruction of homes. Eventually, all was resolved and the highway was built, but with a tremendous impact on the neighbors who had to endure five years of "mud on rainy days, dry dust the rest of the time, and heavy machinery at night."[93] Finally, construction was completed and the official opening held on October 12, 1960.

The park district had been extremely active during the Depression, with further additions and consolidations also occurring during and right after the war. The Mills family had sold their land to the park district for $212,000, and the large Farson house was put to immediate use for a wide variety of community purposes. During the war, the Red Cross had made use of the second floor in support of its activities. There were a lot of changes occasioned by the deaths or resignations of longtime park board members, and a number of the parks were renamed at this time. Along with the combination of liberal and progressive programs came the seemingly typical Oak Park backlash and compromises with concerned neighbors affected by the new facilities and programs. Increasingly vocal complaints came from citizens about noise, danger and the inappropriate use of the parks. As a result, the board created a park district police force in 1942, added the consumption of alcohol to the list of illegal acts and also forbade the playing of hardball in several of the major fields. A major boost to the district was the announcement by Henry Austin Jr. that he would leave his estate, which was the remnant of his family's once vast holdings, to the park district upon the deaths of both himself and his wife. He died in 1947, and his artist wife expressed the hope that the home could be made available to the art league, of which she was a former president. However, when she died in 1964, the building had deteriorated to the point that honoring her request was deemed unrealistic by all concerned.

The other major park-related change in the late 1940s was the decision of the village board and the park district to close Woodbine Avenue between Division and Berkshire Streets to create one large recreational area; later, similar closings removed the need for playground users to cross a street between a school and a playground or a playground and a park. In addition, recognizing the reality of contemporary sports needs, the district allowed for the construction of baseball diamonds on the large park on Woodbine Avenue.[94] Another new park was added when the park district acquired the land that Northern Illinois Gas Company no longer needed for its gas-producing facility south of Garfield Street. Finally, marking the end of an era, the board agreed to allow playgrounds to be opened for use on Sundays.

Though educational issues were not a primary topic of controversy in the immediate postwar period, a general realization was that upgrading and modernization were necessary. The schools were very local in their orientation, covering from kindergarten through the eighth grade, before the children left their neighborhoods to attend the centrally located high school. Paid crossing guards were posted at major intersections, but the decades-old gender-specific way of dealing with the children's movement and behavior remained the same: girl monitors were in charge of hall and stairway traffic, and the eighth-grade patrol boys with their badges controlled the traffic at most street corners. And in Oak Park, in addition to the Parents and Teachers Association, a second group, a Mother's Club, provided enrichment in cultural areas with special services to help the teachers.

But the buildings were getting old, and some had inadequate space for various activities and programs deemed important for their educational value. Science labs were in short supply, and it was hard to find enough space for gym-related activities in the older buildings. The District 97 Board of Education decided to upgrade or replace all of the elementary schools as early as 1950, a project accomplished after the voters approved a large bond issue of about $6,750,000 in a special referendum in 1955. Work began at several schools at a time, and everything was completed by 1960. Some parents thought that the improvements didn't go far enough and that the structure of the schools should be changed to permit larger cohorts of older students and enable specialized classes to be offered. This was the start of both the junior high and middle school movements, but the community provided only minimal support for that kind of change. Many citizens were angered at plans for reorganization and for the construction of new schools so soon after the completion of the upgrades and expansions. Particular ire was directed at the fact that the old Lowell School was unused by the late 1960s, with classrooms lost in the upgrades and fireproofing projects that had been recently completed. Those who believed that education could be furthered and enhanced by a different form of organization would continue to work for change, while those who felt that good education had little to do with the structure of the program opposed all plans for reorganization.

Even more controversy developed over the political structure in the village government. Over the years, in addition to the very poorly received suggestion of being annexed to Chicago, three issues concerning governance kept recurring. The first was the idea of changing the form of government from a village, with a president and trustees elected at large, to an incorporated city, with a mayor and aldermen to represent specific wards or districts. The second was the idea of changing from electing the whole village board at one time instead of electing for staggered terms. The third was the idea of hiring a professional village manager with the responsibility of running the community, thereby decreasing the powers and day-to-day work of the president and board.

The first issue, considered and hotly debated during the first twenty years after disconnection from Cicero Township, was on the ballot and defeated in both 1914 and 1916, with the Oak Park City Form of Government League leading the battle. Occasionally a campaign issue in later years, changing the form of government never surfaced as the deciding matter in a campaign again. Staggered terms not only became an issue but also resulted in changes several times over the years. At first, elections occurred every year, followed by an era of staggered terms and, later still, a push for an election only every four years.

It is difficult to know how much political influence was traded or how much patronage or corruption took place during the early first decades as an independent village, as the election rhetoric and the accuracy of the letters to the editor in support or against any slate of candidates can't be verified. Although most elections were contested, it was in the form of competing nonpartisan slates, and at least in the early years, the candidates kept a low profile about their general party affiliations. In particular, campaign ads and posters identified their professional experience, their public service and, often, their family status but not an identification with either major national party.

After the 1919 election and the temporary victory in throwing the rascals out, the village continued to grow, develop and prosper, but many felt the growth came at the expense of clean government. A typical article in the local press after the election of 1921 indicated no criticism of the way the village was run but gave chills to the reformers. In addition to noting that police officers presented flowers to those elected, the article noted: "Mr. Pyott (the President) was presented with a great silver loving cup by the employe [*sic*] of the various private enterprises of which he is head."[95] The solution, in the minds of reformers, was to support a change to a village manager form of government, with the president and trustees having no say in hiring anyone but the village manager and only approving contracts on the basis of appropriate bidding procedures. A group had run for village office in 1915 as the Primary Association slate, with the aim of moving to a manager form of government. Although the candidates won, they never made any headway in making it happen. Through the late 1930s and the 1940s, the candidates for the village board became more known by their political party identification.

Disgusted with the influence of external political bosses on local affairs, the reformers of the late 1940s were emboldened to push for change while a Cook County grand jury was investigating the ties between the county Republican committeeman from Oak Park, Walter E. McCarron, and the majority members of the Oak Park Village Board. By this time, it was clear which national party held the loyalty of the candidates for local office. Some of the reform leaders had participated in a great book discussion group and decided to try to make major changes, as Oak Park's politics were featured in the Chicago press, along with notes of board meetings that failed for lack of a quorum. The reform group started an organization named Education for Democracy and advocated for reform.[96] Its philosophy was that reform could best be achieved by having a professional village manager, by ending patronage in hiring and the awarding of contracts and by increasing citizen participation in the selection of candidates. In addition, it decided to run a slate in the 1949 election dedicated to those principles of change, though slating the incumbent, President Cochran. A three-way race saw many allegations that its group, the Village Independent Party, had improper signatures on its petitions, in what became a continuous fight against negative ads. The board had no staggered terms at this point, so all of the slots were at stake. The VIP lost, with three Democrats and three Republicans elected as trustees and a Republican as president.

The new board was so fractious that the entire board of health resigned that June, after the village board held its budget hostage while also inserting political hires into the health programs.[97] So little was being accomplished that the board actually voted to meet weekly, hoping to pass at least some legislation. But partisan politics, patronage and corruption continued, with the local press reporting that one of the trustees reported at a board meeting on January 14, 1950, that "Health Department Equipment and Personnel had spent a day making Photostats of election petitions for Walter E. McCarron, candidate for re-election as Republican Township Committeeman." The Republican village president Robert F. Gaesel was then quoted as saying that he saw nothing wrong with that, as the staff did it on their own time.[98] Typically, the response to the issue split along party lines, and the Democrats on the board found nothing strange in Thomas A. Walpole concurrently holding the positions of Democratic committeeman, township assessor and village corporate counsel.

Though they had lost the 1949 election, the Education for Democracy leadership got a major boost when the Illinois General Assembly passed a law in 1951 that would allow municipalities to adopt a village manager form of government by referendum. So, the leadership of Dwight Follett, Cyrus Giddings, Arthur Thorpe (later the village attorney) and others shifted gears and founded a new group, the Village Manager Association (VMA), to examine the possibility of establishing a manager form of government in Oak Park. Working with committees, going door to door and inviting neighbors for coffee, the group managed to get many more signatures than the 2,300 necessary to place the question "Shall Oak Park Adopt a Managerial Form of Government?" on the November ballot. The effort was so strong and visible that the Chicago newspapers even re   ported on the progress of the campaign and the local chamber of commerce got on board in support. Using the same process of personal contact and meeting with community groups, the VMA was also aided by the actions of the sitting board when its members petulantly refused to attend a meeting to allocate funds for the special referendum ballots.

The election of November 4, 1952, produced the highest turnout of any in the history of the village, with nobody even running for the board, and the

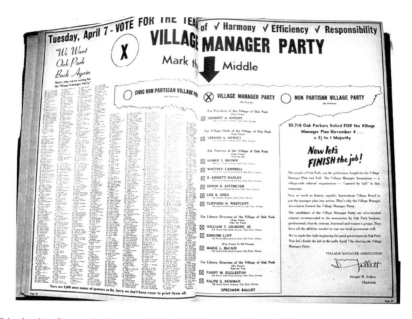

This election flyer and ad not only identified the candidates of the village manager party but also made a strong pitch for completing the revolution begun with the vote to establish the village manager form of government. *Courtesy of HSOPRF.*

referendum was approved by a more than three-to-one margin. With only five months until the April 1953 election, and with momentum on the side of reform, the group set up a process for attracting people to run for the seats of president, clerk and trustee. Having worked hard to unseat machine-supported candidates, the group decided not to run any of its leaders. Ads were placed, people were canvassed and community groups were asked to identify possible candidates. More than 750 citizens and one hundred organizations responded, and a selection committee was appointed to screen candidates and select a slate.

Though the process had reached out to many people and groups, the chosen slate consisted entirely of white professional men, though the VMA-backed candidates for the library board included women. A massive campaign ensued, with another three-way race for the village board. The VMA slate placed ads in both the local and Chicago newspapers and on radio and mailed thousands of pieces of literature supporting its candidates and the concepts for which they stood. This time, the reformers elected their candidates for president, clerk and all six trustees. The victorious group took office and hired Mark Keane as the first village manager. The McCarron group ran again in 1957 but lost badly, ending the externally controlled machine politics in Oak Park. As proof of the new order, as Keane recalled later, he received a manila envelope filled with parking tickets from an Oak Park business owner, with the expectation that the manager would void them. "We don't do that anymore," Keane replied in a note.[99] Yet old habits died hard, and it took a while for everyone to believe that the village board was going to let the manager manage.

The VMA process—with wide citizen involvement in nominating and supporting candidates but keeping hands off once candidates for office were elected—had its problems and critics. Almost everyone believed that a cleaner government was now the norm. However, in view of the lack of primaries associated with the nonpartisan selection process, this caused some members of the community to feel that the new VMA, which continued to win most elections for years to come, failed to see that elections reflected the most democratic method. So, once again, progressive ideas of reform created issues about the preservation of control by the elite.

By the mid-1950s, many of the congregations of the major Protestant denominations had grown in size, with newer and sometimes larger church structures to house them. Battles against the creation of the Roman Catholic churches were over; they had all been built. The Jewish community became the next group to experience discrimination and the antipathy of their neighbors. Jews of various levels of orthodoxy resided in the community by the 1920s, and all worshiped at synagogues or rented halls outside Oak Park. Then, in 1934, a group that identified with the conservative movement received a charter to found the West Suburban Jewish Community Center, with services run by the laity. It may have been this group that tried to buy the building that became the Dole Library but ended up renting a storefront on Madison Street, east of Harlem, for its devotions and as a religious school. The group then purchased and remodeled the building at 414 Lake Street for use as a synagogue.

The congregation grew and sought to enlarge the structure. However, a village ordinance required the consent of more than half of the neighbors within a radius of four hundred feet to approve the expansion, but the neighbors were not willing to support the congregation. Wartime material and labor shortages limited all civilian construction, thus making the issue moot for the duration. At war's end, the congregation grew dramatically, as many Jewish families left Chicago for the suburbs, with many moving to Oak Park.[100] By 1950, almost three hundred families were members of the congregation, and the earlier expansion plan would no longer meet the increased needs. So, finding no congenial solution in Oak Park, members of the congregation looked to adjacent River Forest, eventually erecting their temple there after overcoming legal and neighborhood opposition.

After renting space for services and religious school at various sites, and wary because of the experience of another synagogue attempting to build in the village, Oak Park Temple used a "straw buyer" to obtain the site and opened in 1957. *Courtesy of the author.*

The reform congregation had a different, but no less problematic, odyssey as its congregants also moved from the area around their substantial building on the West Side of Chicago. In the early stages of planning to move, the congregation established several satellite facilities in rented space, with Sunday school classes at Holmes School at first, followed by Mann School, while other programs were run in buildings in the Chicago Galewood community and in the nearby suburb of Elmwood Park. Having learned from the negative reaction of neighbors to the plans of the conservative group, the congregation resorted to the strategy of utilizing a "straw buyer" to acquire the desired property. The building was constructed on Harlem Avenue, and the first services were held in 1957. The rabbi, Leonard Mervis, asked to join the Council of Churches, which had been founded in the 1930s and was composed entirely of Protestant congregations. He was rebuffed, as were the overtures of the Catholic churches, but he was told that the council would be happy to send him the minutes of its meetings.

One of the bigger changes to affect the lives of hundreds of villagers by the end of the 1950s was the end of the Yaryan heating system. Not only did the system not reach more than the old core of town, it had also never been effective in heating the upper floors of homes. As a result, many homes already had boilers or furnaces of one sort or another to supplement the heat that ran through the hot-water pipes. The Illinois Commerce Commission gave permission to discontinue the system in 1956, and by the time it actually ceased operations in 1958, it was using three hundred tons of coal a day to operate the system to serve fewer than six hundred customers. The company donated the land it had occupied to the village in 1963, when the village manager reported that the cost to take down the building and concrete chimney would be $32,000 and that a parking lot would replace the structures, at least temporarily. The village incinerator was located near the Yaryan plant, and it had become clear that the way garbage was being burned created even more pollution than the utility's stack, so the incinerator was closed and removed, with all trash now going to a landfill.

The village continued to prosper during this postwar period, with a lot of income continuing to flow from the sales generated by the local department stores and car dealerships, enabling the village to upgrade the lighting system, do a lot of road and sewer work and make real progress on the paving of alleys. This last issue was not one-sided, as many citizens either worried about increased traffic and speeding on paved alleys or objected to assessments to pay for the work, or both.

This field house, named for Hans Christian Anderson, was designed by Prairie School architect John van Bergen in 1926 and underwent updating in the mid-1950s. *Courtesy of Park District of Oak Park.*

The park district was at least as active as the village in this era, also updating the lighting system in Austin Gardens and making improvements to the conservatory and various field houses. A lot of attention was paid to Mills Park and the Farson Home, which was now a community house within the district. Park district minutes of that era are replete with requests to use the house by many organizations and for a number of purposes, including the use of the second floor for a senior day center. This was agreed to in 1956, at first on a trial basis of three days a week. Details of complex and even unusual requests for the use of park facilities became a feature of most meetings, with the park board agreeing in 1958 to allow Boy Scouts to use a pistol range to help qualify for a marksman merit badge. Approval was granted on condition of a fee payment and the Scouts' carrying insurance.

One new community amenity long under discussion had been the creation of a combined swimming pool and ice skating rink for the community. All swimming and swimming lessons were confined to those having memberships at the Oak Park Country Club, the YMCA or the Nineteenth Century Woman's Club, though the latter offered swimming lessons to nonmembers for a modest fee. The park board began the process of exploring the costs of pools and skating rinks in June 1960. An investigating committee made up of members of various service organizations reported back in favor of these facilities and recommended a recreational site at Ridgeland Common.

After the usual "not in my backyard" objections were overruled, the facility was opened in the summer of 1962 to general acclaim and high usage, followed by Rehm Pool. However, the plastic identification cards used as pool passes soon created a problem, as a June 3 report indicated that a May teen festival in Austin Gardens required the entire Oak Park police force to enforce order. Moreover, it was discovered that 70 percent of the teens with ID passes lived neither in Oak Park nor River Forest. Steps to control access were soon taken, and the problems abated.

The other major public works project of the early 1960s was the construction of a new and expanded main public library. For many years after a study committee by the director of the Detroit Public Library found the Scoville Institute Building to be inadequate and even unsafe, there was both strong sentiment to keep the landmark building and fears directed at the cost of a major new structure. Such fears made passage of a referendum in favor of a bond issue difficult for more than twenty years, but one finally passed on the third attempt in 1961. The firm of Holabird and Root was hired to construct the building, favoring an open design for "future flexibility," and the more than $1,000,000 building was opened in 1964. An annual Village Art Fair had been held, usually on a closed Marion Street between Lake and Ontario Streets since 1955. As part of the fair's activities, the first outdoor public sculpture to be commissioned since the dedication of the Peace Memorial was selected as the result of a national competition run by the fair and was placed next to the entrance to the library.

Cultural activities continued unabated in the postwar period, with changes primarily in regard to venue and professionalism. The symphony continued to attract Chicago Symphony Orchestra members, though a racial incident in 1963 caused an uproar when a black performer sat in at a rehearsal. The comments of the president of the Oak Park Symphony Association drove both the black violinist and the Jewish conductor away, and the orchestra had to find a new conductor.

Various groups offered summer concerts at Ridgeland Common in the 1960s, including the local orchestra and several choral groups. Founded in 1943, the Oak Park Barbershop Chorus won the Illinois State Championship in competition in 1955. The group headed off to the national competition in Florida that year, vowing to come back and update the slogan for Oak Park from "World's Largest Village" to "World's Largest and Most Harmonious Village."[101] Unfortunately, the group finished only fourth in the competition. With a longer run, the Village Players theater troupe opened in a rented facility in 1959, utilizing local actors, with a core of dedicated troupe members as the mainstay, through the first two decades. Long in a rented space on South Boulevard, presenting a combination of classics, melodramas, musicals and more contemporary material, the Village Players finally were able to raise the funds to purchase and adapt a building to its use on Madison Street in 1984.

Starting in 1964, and under discussion for the next several years, was the possibility of a merger of the park district and the village playground program, then part of the renamed village recreation department. The League of Women Voters weighed in, suggesting that an exploration of the idea be undertaken. Other aspects of dealing with both facility needs and the growth and demands of new programs occupied much of the park board's time through the mid-1960s. Nothing happened at that time, but a Recreation in the Streets program was started in 1965. Unfortunately, teen vandalism remained a pressing issue in the community, and the parks and park facilities were favorite targets. Exasperated sufficiently, the park board asked the village police chief for approval of an eleven-person park patrol, with the goal of recruiting others to patrol the parks and report illegal activities.[102] Obviously, not all youth were getting into trouble, and the village board was happy to note and recognize the Oak Park Boys Baseball Team for winning the 1968

Bronco League World (national) championship, during an era in which the high school often won regional and state titles in a number of sports.

While access to recreation and tolerance of diversity got occasional press attention, traffic and parking were on everyone's minds once wartime scarcity was a thing of the past. Not only had the last horse-drawn vehicles been retired, but the ready availability of all the major automobile dealerships in the community, and the growth of credit, also made car ownership all but a craze. The local press was filled with editorials on the subject of parking, letters also took up the theme and the police were concerned about the increase in the number of accidents and even fatalities as the population hovered at about seventy thousand. In the late 1940s, the village had taken a first step to provide off-street parking by purchasing a lot large enough to accommodate fifty cars. However, in 1950, the then village president oversaw the sale of the lot, stating: "The purchase was ill-advised from the outset." The *Oak Leaves* retort was withering, for it noted the need for parking and pointed out the irony that the president had been the comptroller when the lot was bought in the first place.[103]

Not surprisingly, the merchants along Madison and Lake Streets, and on Oak Park Avenue, were most concerned, with the former suggesting that diagonal parking be instituted. In 1968, the village board directed staff to examine the possibility of creating a service drive along Madison Street, with parking on both sides of the drive, but the combination of width issues and the need to access driveways where no alley access existed made that option impossible. Greater attention was being paid to alley paving as well, but that would have called for special assessments, and neighbors often came down on different sides of the paving issue.

From time to time, there had been intermittent talk, since the end of World War II, about changing the structure of Elementary School District 97 to develop the kind of seventh- and eighth-grade junior high system that existed in other places around the country, but nobody had taken the issue very far. However, the district board appointed and asked a new superintendent to do a study to determine the feasibility of setting up such a junior high system—the assumption was that there would be one school on the north side of the village and one on the south.[104] Supporters felt there could be greater specialization at a lower cost, quality teaching and ability grouping available by virtue of the mass of students. Detractors opposed the plan as being too expensive, as taking away the neighborhood school that had stood the test of time and as creating a need for lunchrooms and questioning who would serve as crossing guards for the younger children if the older ones did not attend the same schools.

In February 1963, the board voted unanimously in favor of setting up Longfellow and Whittier Schools as junior highs. Anger over the decision was immediate and strong, and more than ten thousand people signed petitions demanding a referendum for that June. There was also strong support for three school board candidates who opposed the change. The anti forces won all three seats by a two-to-one majority, with nine times as many people voting as in the previous election. The Illinois attorney general ruled that the requested referendum would be only advisory, but the new board made this a moot question by dropping the plan.

Another issue of tremendous impact on the entire community was the initial, stunning devastation of the Dutch elm disease that hit the area about 1960 and soon was wreaking havoc along the streets of the community, in the parks and on private property. Although the forestry department initiated a spirited battle, very little was known at first about the best way to combat the disease, and whole streets lost the beautiful arboreal archways that had come to be a hallmark of the community. At this point in time, taking down the trees at the first sign of infection seemed the best way to go, and that was done. Later, in the 1960s, trimming and spraying were also tried, and more draconian measures were instituted still later.

The middle of the 1960s was one of the most dramatic eras in the village's history, as the whole issue of open housing and access to both the sale and rental market for African Americans came to a head. African Americans had actually decreased in number in the community since the closing of Mount Carmel Baptist Church and the urban renewal that preceded the construction of the Westgate complex. Only about seventy-five persons of color were counted at mid-century, with no institutions with which they were identified then existing. Scattered throughout the community, African Americans, for the most part, were not in very high-profile or prestigious positions, though a respected and accomplished black scientist had lived in the village without attracting much attention since 1947.[105] When Dr. Percy Julian and his family moved into a very large and expensive house in the most affluent part of town, there was trouble almost immediately. Even before the family moved in, there was an attempt to torch the house while renovations were being made. Later, there was a dynamite attack, and there were also threats made by letter and phone. Many supporters rallied to the Julians' defense, and prominent citizens not only went on record as supporting the family's right to live there but also made real overtures of friendship. Many have suggested that the prominent Julian family was a far greater threat to their persecutors than were people the bigots could look down on as their educational or social inferiors. The incidents kept the Julian family cut off from full participation in the community, showing that racism was still a potent toxin in Oak Park. Over the next few years, a few other black families moved into homes, but the basic climate and complexion of the community remained the same. Only toward the end of the 1950s did the suggestion of change really occur.

Racial change on the West Side of Chicago started to exert more pressure on blacks who wanted greater choices in housing. Close-in communities like Oak Park were the only places remotely available to them, offering ease of transportation to downtown Chicago; a wide choice of rental apartments, condos and single-family homes; and proximity to family and churches nearby. Consequently, aware of the problems of the Julian family and the overtly racist comments of those who feared racial change, new black families who wanted to move to Oak Park found the climate essentially worse. Through the late 1950s, the number of new black families who settled in Oak Park was tiny, and the homes were usually bought through nominees. However, greater attention to race and housing was on the minds of Oak Park's liberal clergy. Local chapters of the National Conference of Christians and Jews and Home Opportunities Made Equal, Inc., were active, holding meetings in the homes of members. In February 1960, a large town hall meeting at First Congregational Church had religious and civil rights leaders speak on behalf of integration and an open-door policy in every community.

The village government became active in responding to the tension, recognizing that there was rapid racial change in Chicago and the need to respect the rule of law in a variety of ways. Harris Stevens, the proactive village manager, and Police Chief Fremont Nester sent notices of the impending moves of African American families to their future neighbors, giving the background of the new families and asking for support and welcoming. Both men also provided their telephone numbers to both the new arrivals and neighbors, asking that they be contacted if there were any problems. Although these well-meaning gestures helped to smooth the reception of the pioneer new families, who were happy to receive such support, they also indicated that blacks couldn't just move in as simply as a white family could. As a recent book on the experience of African Americans in Oak Park noted: "The black residents knew nothing of their new neighbors' education, ages, or occupations, while the white neighbors had a summary of the personal and professional accomplishments of their new black neighbors."[106] Nonetheless, the new families arrived, their children were enrolled in Oak Park's schools and many joined local churches and other community organizations; there was no turning back.

Chapter 9

THE QUEST FOR RACIAL AND ECONOMIC DIVERSITY

Not everyone was in favor of change in the community, and those who were might have had competing thoughts both on what change was desirable and how change might be managed. However, the elected officials of all the major boards seemed to be willing to face new realities and even (in many arenas) plan for them. Most active in trying to anticipate needs and solutions, the village board challenged its planning committee to make suggestions as to how to improve Oak Park. The committee reported back in December 1965 with several recommendations. Addressing the problems associated with decay and the ever-increasing problem of parking, especially along the corridors of large, older apartment houses, the commission suggested that the village provide off-street parking.

Going further, it also noted that some buildings were substandard or nonconforming in their areas and suggested that the village purchase those properties and either see to their repair or demolish them to provide for parking. Addressing its perception of insufficient play areas for younger children, the commission suggested that the village actively acquire land for playgrounds. Noting that much attention had always been paid to traffic issues, the regulation of traffic via signage and adjustments to speed limits, the commission asked the board to review the street pattern, with no limitations on the scope of such a review. Finally, addressing the often-expressed concerns of the public safety leadership and others who decried the far-flung locations of the centers of public services and the homes of the various taxing bodies, the commission's last recommendation was that the

The large courtyard apartment houses that were built along Washington and Austin Boulevards in the 1920s were designed to provide the maximum amount of light and air possible. The protruding sun porches also permit cross-ventilation, and the parapet hides the flat roof. *Courtesy of the author.*

community might well benefit from the construction of a new civic center. All of these issues were part of the community dialogue for the next several decades, with some matters addressed and, to a large degree, resolved. Others remained at the core of policy and legislation.

At the same time, the West Side of Chicago was undergoing rapid racial change, and there was disinvestment in the community, as second and third rings of suburbs were expanding out beyond the older, established towns. While there was, at first, a positive impact of the newcomers in the western suburbs on the business community of Oak Park, the fact that new shopping centers like North Riverside Plaza and the Oakbrook Mall both opened in the early 1960s ultimately had a more profound and negative impact on Oak Park's economic base. The major Oak Park department stores didn't close at that time, but the existence of those malls siphoned off many of the shoppers from the western and southern suburbs who previously had done their major shopping in the village. At the same time, the availability of new markets in the outer suburbs and the availability of large areas of cheap land precipitated an exodus of the automobile dealers from Madison Street's Automobile Row. This process started a bit later than the early malls, and went more slowly, but it had just as deleterious an impact on the community's tax base.

The merchants along Madison Street had long demanded the easing of parking restrictions on nearby streets. But the old familiar concerns expressed by the residents of the single-family homes were that parking lots on their blocks would be a violation of zoning and that allowing on-street parking for shoppers and employees of the stores would ruin the character of their suburban neighborhood and lower their property values. Neighbors feared that allowing any lots south of Madison, under a comprehensive zoning amendment adopted in 1966, would be the opening round that would result in the loss of their homes. Yet with the depth of commercial lots being so shallow and an alley separating their businesses from areas zoned single-family residential, the merchants had nowhere to go to either expand their businesses or provide much-needed parking.

The problem was particularly severe for the car dealers as shopping habits changed. Up to that time, the prospective buyer decided what kind of car was wanted, visited a showroom on Madison or Lake Streets, or Roosevelt Road, examined the models displayed, made a decision and ordered the car with the desired options for later delivery. With larger spaces available in the exurbs, the automobile dealers operating there could stock a large variety of cars, eliminating the frustrations and disappointments of ordering and enabling the customer to drive home with a new car on the day of purchase. Given the prices of Oak Park property compared to the prices in the newly opened areas, it is probable that the exodus of car dealers would have happened even if zoning and neighbors had been willing to allow business expansion into the adjacent areas. However, the resistance to change and compromise certainly accelerated the process.

The park district and the village recreation department continued to develop facilities and programs through the 1960s, even after the major successes in opening the two water complexes. A tot lot at Randolph and Grove was added in 1965, and both Barrie and Rehm Playgrounds were renovated. Construction began on new recreation center buildings at Fox, Longfellow and Stevenson Parks. Several of these projects were undertaken by the recreation department after the park district transferred underutilized land to the village. As an exercise in cooperation and fiscal prudence, the park district requested that the village police patrol the parks instead of having to maintain a separate park unit. Further enhancing opportunities for children, the Recreation in the Streets program began in 1965, with traveling equipment, sponsored games and crafts and facilities to bring to the very popular summer block parties. There was overlap of mission, to some extent, between the park and village boards, but these initiatives helped to address the planning committee recommendation mentioned earlier.

In the 1970s, the village's recreation department equipped traveling playgrounds, visiting block parties and community-wide celebrations. The portable facilities contained games for both active and passive sports, and a trained staff worked with the children. *Courtesy of Park District of Oak Park.*

Meanwhile, the pros and cons of racial diversity remained the stuff of newspaper headlines. As the diversity topic was inexorably tied to what was happening in neighboring Austin, the response to the pressures for housing in Oak Park and the implications of becoming a diverse community became the major focus of public debate. Coupled with the then existing reality of economic changes and the erosion of the sales tax base, the word "diversity" took on even more meaning, and obtaining and maintaining economic and racial diversity became the twin pillars of public policy.

Through the early 1960s—at the same time that the West Side of Chicago was experiencing block-by-block resegregation and panic peddling, along with the related practices of unscrupulous real estate brokers in full force—a modest number of black families continued to buy homes in the village, primarily through nominees. The practice was supported by such organizations as the Housing Committee of the Citizens Committee for Human Rights. As real estate interests opposed any open housing legislation at either the state or local level and supported the right of a homeowner to refuse to sell to a minority buyer, open housing advocates felt that they had no choice but to resort to the subterfuge of the straw buyer. The Oak Park

Board of Realtors was so negative that it unanimously passed a resolution opposing the proposed legislation when the state was considering an open housing bill under state legislative consideration in the spring of 1965.

Frustrated by real estate negativity and resistance by a segment of the community but emboldened by the success and generally favorable reaction of neighbors to the new residents, once they had moved in, the Citizens Committee for Human Rights started a more active program of recruiting, welcoming and conducting tours for African American families to help them identify prospective places to live. Various demonstrations, marches, speeches before the village board and community meetings occurred at the same time that increased civil rights activities were taking place in Chicago. There was often cooperation and cross participation between the Oak Park and Chicago groups. Not surprisingly, the open housing supporters often found it easier to get a family into a home than an apartment, as landlords were afraid that the white tenants would leave if a black tenant moved in.

In response to speeches in favor of an open housing ordinance, in July 1966 the village president responded that until the Illinois Supreme Court ruled on the matter, the legality of such an ordinance was in doubt, but he referred the issue to the Community Relations Commission. Several months later, however, the board took an active step toward dealing with panic peddling and other negative practices by passing an antisolicitation ordinance that clearly spoke to the issue of soliciting sales by stating or implying that "the property has been, or is about to be reduced in value by reason of the race, color or religion of persons who have or may move into the vicinity of the property involved."[107]

Anti–open housing sentiment was vocal and substantial, though nuanced. Some critics of access were openly racist, citing crime statistics and the inappropriateness of mixing of the races and expressing their belief in black inferiority. Others spoke to creating access for all but opposed the intrusion of either the legislature or the village board in requiring homeowners to sell to anyone and diminishing their property rights.

In the 1965 elections for the village and library boards, the Preserve Oak Park Party ran a full slate of candidates who stressed their church affiliations and large families in their campaign literature and who were anti–open housing. The public debate sharpened, intensified and became more strident through the end of 1966 and through early 1968, when more than ten thousand Oak Park residents signed and delivered a petition to the village board, requesting a referendum before any open or fair housing legislation was approved. The village board felt that it had the authority to act without an advisory referendum, as it believed that it was doing what was both legally and morally correct. The board passed its landmark ordinance, now with the support of the local real estate community, in April 1968. Supporters of the referendum went to court, but the issue never went to trial. The village attorney, Arthur Thorpe, citing a U.S. Supreme Court case of 1866 that stated that blacks have the right to rent or buy property, noted that the village was responding to the issue of open housing but only 102 years too late.[108]

While the linkage of African Americans with criminal activities had been one of the motifs of opponents of open housing, crime itself was becoming a bigger issue than in previous eras, with particular growth in the arena of juvenile crime. Some concerns were drug related, though mostly of the minor variety. The high school superintendent helped prompt the village board to amend an ordinance to ban the sale of glue that some youths were sniffing. Spray-painted graffiti was also a concern in the mid-1960s, but less so than thefts from unlocked automobiles and garages. The press reported crime statistics and the details of the more sensational or even humorous actions. Both new and used car lots were tempting, and one story recounted how three very young teenagers had stolen a car from a lot, driven it around until it ran out of gas and then returned to the car lot and taken another one before being apprehended. The first juvenile officer was added to the police department in 1966 to comply with a state mandate, yet juvenile crime increased threefold between that year and 1968.

Very few of these crimes were directed against a person, but the concern prompted several courses of action around that time. First, the Oak Park trustees met with their township counterparts and the juvenile police officer to discuss programs to combat crime; there was also discussion of forming a juvenile police corps. A disorderly conduct ordinance was passed in 1969. It was not aimed specifically against teenage groups congregating but was thought of in those terms by some, and the village board was forced to amend the ordinance several months later in that it raised constitutional issues relating to free assembly and peaceful protest.

Housing issues were not only focused on race. For example, the earlier resistance to the dangers of large apartment houses was rekindled whenever a building started to fall into disrepair. The 1965 planning committee report had addressed the need for parking and the problems of obsolescence, but the village board felt the need to discuss the possible inspection of all buildings before their sale could be finalized.[109] Parking remained a huge and growing problem, even though many of the newer apartment houses built in the 1960s were condominiums, with on-site parking for an upscale market. Residents in the older buildings had no place to park in an era of expanding automobile ownership. Also, older buildings, to be competitive in attracting tenants with financial means, found it difficult when the tenants would have to make the effort to find their own parking. Thus, fearing that they were increasingly fighting a losing battle and worried about the potential of increased pressure from prospective black renters, the owners of these older buildings were strongly supportive of any plans that would address the parking issues. Yet, at the same time, the police department supported the on-street parking ban as a deterrent to crime, limiting the possibility of someone jumping a pedestrian from between parked cars at night.

With many of the issues facing the village overlapping and having been referenced in the report of the planning committee in 1965, the village started to move toward the development of a comprehensive plan late in 1967. A planning consultant was hired for a preliminary study, and the village board quickly moved toward a commitment to both the creation of a plan and turning the planning committee into a regularly functioning commission with statutory powers consistent with making recommendations to the village board on the adoption of a plan. With the help of the Citizens Action Committee, a plan was developed with widespread citizen input and discussion. The final report was completed by the Department of Planning and Development and adopted in 1973. Later, in 1979, the comprehensive plan turned the approaches and goals of the first version into the articulation of a set of policies to lead planning in the village.

As part of the planning study, a questionnaire was developed and distributed widely that contained several key elements that provided citizen response to the original planning study. First of all, the study showed no support for on-street parking and reaffirmed all of the negative reactions to shared parking or expansion of business parking into the residential neighborhoods. Similarly rejected was any further density to be achieved by allowing high-rise apartment houses. Additionally, there was fairly strong opposition to the creation of a civic center, but that appeared to be in response to the probable or expected cost of such a building project. Through these responses, the community again showed itself to be progressive in thinking about and planning for the future but unwilling to see many changes in the most problematic areas for which the professionals were calling for new approaches.

Good intentions in planning, public policy regarding open housing and maintaining an alert police force were insufficient to deal with many of the primary issues the village was so rapidly facing. As a result, the various taxing bodies began to work proactively and in partnership with a number of private and not-for-profit organizations to develop meaningful and effective tools and programs to combat the mortgage redlining and panic peddling that were beginning to plague the community, to provide open housing without falling into classic patterns of resegregation and to stimulate economic development despite the increasing loss of sales tax revenue from diminished retail and automobile sales. An extremely large set of programs and initiatives was established in the early to mid-1970s, many of which formed the bedrock of both public and private civic and commercial efforts to move the village to and through the next stages of its development. Many of these efforts also flew in the face of citizen responses to the planning process questionnaire.

A major overhaul of the village's lighting system had been under discussion, and was given tacit approval, in the late 1960s. However, the substantial questions relating to both cost and design took years to resolve. Finally, a new comprehensive lighting system was approved, utilizing the old fixtures with newer, brighter lights on the side streets and adding overhanging bright lights to the major arteries. Many staff favored the use of the sodium vapor lights utilized by Chicago, but the citizenry wanted a softer light color, even at the price of some lost efficiency. Before the change, the light level was so low that it was very difficult to see the identifying addresses painted on homes, and there was a widespread belief that brighter light would also be a deterrent to crime. In its broader application, the issue of better lighting also addressed one of the issues in the report of the original planning committee.

A minor lighting issue was the height and density of the trees on residential streets. Dutch elm disease continued to have a powerful impact, and in 1969 alone more than five hundred trees were removed. About eighteen thousand were sprayed in what was increasingly becoming a rear-guard action, slowing the spread of the blight but having no real hope of saving any of the elms. Budgetary concerns were also growing as the more aggressive Oak Park programs put the costs of tree work higher than the cost for those communities that were more content to just take down the trees when they died, but the program continued. By 1969, the forestry staff was working on Saturdays, as well as during the normal workweek, removing infected trees and setting up a plan to have no more than 10 percent of any one kind of tree on a given block. Further, and most drastically, to get down all infected trees as soon as they were identified, the village took on the police power to remove infected trees from private property if the owners didn't respond quickly enough to notification. Owners were then

Cul-de-sacs like this one at Austin Boulevard and Van Buren Street were designed to provide much needed parking in areas with high-density older apartments that had no parking available. Though criticized as cutting Oak Park off from Chicago, other internal cul-de-sacs and street closings were added through the 1980s. *Courtesy of the author.*

billed, and a lien was placed on their property if they refused to pay.[110] Given the way the infection spread, such action was necessary and helped slow the demise of all elms, though as many as 1,500 were lost each year in the late 1960s and early 1970s.

The installation of cul-de-sac streets also addressed two other issues in the planning committee's document: the need for parking in the older apartment areas and updating the street pattern. With that justification, the village board approved a series of cul-de-sacs and outright street closings, especially along Austin Boulevard, starting with those completed by the summer of 1974. The cul-de-sacs contained on-street parking that the village felt could be defended without breaking the ban on on-street parking, as they became parking enclaves. Though the cul-de-sacs achieved the desired end of servicing the parking needs of the buildings along one of the major apartment house arterials, critics complained that the closings were being used to keep blacks out of Oak Park.[111] The accusation persists, and may or may not be accurate, but the efficacy of such a tool found favor in other parts of the village, where parking issues were perceived as dire. Cul-de-sacs also became part of traffic diversion efforts and providing parking in areas far from apartment houses, especially on the edge of business districts.

Other related parking issues included the continued opposition of residents to aspects of the Comprehensive Zoning Amendment of 1966, as they feared that the amendment could be used as the leading edge of a thrust into business parking lots in their neighborhoods, particularly south of Madison Street and south of North Avenue. How to accommodate shoppers' cars along Madison, and at the medical and other offices on the Oak Park side of North, was the issue in common, and the concern and opposition was identical. However, at the end of 1969, the village board pushed ahead and unanimously approved the creation of special use–parking lots that allowed business-related parking during the day and resident parking at night. The village manager suggested that the board consider multilevel parking garages in its deliberations on parking. He also said that he felt that a study of that subject was in order, a suggestion that quickly evolved into a board commitment to funding a consultant to do an overall space study.

Another issue related to the earlier planning committee's recommendation regarding housing involved the development and growth of the Oak Park Residence Corporation, which had been formed in 1966 and was increasingly active in acquiring and rehabilitating substandard apartment buildings throughout the village. Working together with the long-established Housing Authority, the Residence Corporation played an important role in expanding the availability of housing for seniors, the disabled and lower-income people in support of its mission to provide and preserve quality and affordable shelter. Such efforts helped to keep the pressure on other apartment building owners to better maintain and upgrade their properties.

More specific and pointed programs to promote diversity were developed and put into place. Working along parallel lines, the not-for-profit Oak Park Housing Center, which local activist Roberta Raymond established at First Congregational Church in 1972, and the village's recently staffed Community Relations Department shared the avowed goal of making Oak Park open to all. This was to be accomplished by avoiding the classic Chicago (and American) pattern of exclusion, panic peddling, redlining, white flight and resegregation, with counseling for both blacks and whites who were contemplating a move to Oak Park. Raymond noted: "For, as long as there exist white enclaves, it will be difficult for Oak Park and other suburbs to achieve integration."[112]

Housing Center supporters also publicly defended the village's counseling program, explaining the need to engage in positive counseling for maintaining integration, preferring to have an upfront program and defending it to achieve the desired end. The village board took a very public and dramatic stance when it passed legislation forbidding the use of "for sale" or "for rent" signs for any residential property, except for limited open house events, in February 1972. The U.S. Supreme Court later held that kind of restriction

The Oak Park (now Oak Park Regional) Housing Center started with a simple plan to peacefully integrate all neighborhoods in Oak Park but now explores a wider circle of communities with its minority clientele and markets its services through a variety of media. *Courtesy of Oak Park Regional Housing Center.*

unconstitutional, but the Oak Park Board of Realtors had become convinced of the value of supporting the concept of a diverse community. As a group, it has voluntarily complied with the prohibition since then.

On a less official level, but completely supported by the village government starting in 1968, were block (or 100, reflecting the north–south numbering system) clubs, including some with the structure of a block captain and other leadership positions. At their peak in 1972, about four hundred of the nearly five hundred blocks in Oak Park had a block club, even though many were inactive.[113] Their roles were to provide information, serve as a conduit between citizens and the government, build community and dispel rumors. Block parties were held during the summer months, with the streets closed, and some blocks also started to organize progressive dinners, hold joint yard sales and develop other ways of getting to know one another and share.

Some blocks concentrated on local community building, while others joined in pressuring the village to provide resources to serve as a conduit of complaints and sometimes back candidates for public office. Unlike other groups of citizens who challenged the local authorities and could be written off as disaffected agitators or cranks, the block clubs had been formed with the blessing of the village. So, when their representatives testified on an issue at village hall, they were treated with respect and found the board most likely to respond publicly in a positive way. The Oak Park Community Organization (founded as Oak Park Citizen's Action Program) had many of the same goals as other groups but was more vocal, activist and confrontational than the representatives of the block clubs, the official village programs or the Housing Center, though many of the same people participated in one or more of the groups.

This photo was taken at the dedication of a newly bricked street on South Humphrey Street in 2007, but to the children, a closed-off street is a block party, with refreshments, games and the chance to run and ride. *Courtesy of the Village of Oak Park.*

Other voluntary citizen organizations, the Hawthorne and Beye Community Councils, were founded in the mid-1970s under the aegis of the neighborhood schools and supported by the administration of each school. Both were concerned with the total success of their communities, education, housing and economic development. The Hawthorne Council was somewhat more organized, with officers and an office donated by Good Shepherd Lutheran Church, and hosted programs to address issues like redlining and community disinvestment. The organization had no paid staff, but there were services provided by the Community Relations Department staff and its graduate school interns. Several of the active members of the council became heavily involved in its activities and later went on to hold public office. The Harrison Street Neighborhood Association started a little later, had similar aims and had part-time staff funded by a grant.

At the other end of the activism spectrum, but equally dedicated to the preservation of the community, its values, ideals and structure, was the creation of the reborn historical society in 1968, founded by a group of laypersons and professionals who were interested in documenting the history of the village and neighboring River Forest, the achievements of native and adopted sons and daughters and the preservation of the past for the future.

With a tripartite mission of collecting, display and enrichment through archives, museum and research center activities, the society moved in 1970 to the second floor of the Farson-Mills Home, where it displayed historic photos and memorabilia, aimed at building pride in the community while educating visitors about the past. Also, with an eye toward recognizing the past accomplishment of a major local figure while preserving his legacy was the establishment of the Frank Lloyd Wright Home and Studio Foundation in 1974 and its acquisition and co-stewardship of the building itself.

Similarly, "Day in Our Village," an annual celebration of Oak Park's organizations, programs and cultural activities, was started in 1973. At various and sometimes multiple locations during the first few years, this event became centered at Scoville Park as a large open space close to the center of the village. Not only have many musical groups performed, food has also been sold and served and games and educational programming, religious organizations, businesses and political groups all continue to set up their booths and distribute their material.

Perhaps the strongest statement in the belief that the village could exist and prosper as a diverse community and combat the fears of those who were writing off the east part of town as "east of Ridgeland" was the final decision concerning what to do about the long-debated planning committee's

"Day in our Village" is held every year in early summer. At first spread throughout the village, entertainment, games for children, food, booths and community information kiosks now fill up Scoville Park. *Courtesy of the Village of Oak Park.*

recommendation that a civic center be constructed. As finances were starting to get very tight with the erosion of the tax base, grand plans for the civic center fell by the wayside, and the village board concentrated on a plan that would bring a new and expanded village hall into being, incorporating as many of the scattered village functions as possible under one roof. Highly visible and somewhat controversial, the decision was made to build in the east-central part of the village rather than near the center of town, along the Lake Street spine on which the then original village hall, post office, library and high school were all housed.

Though the placement along Madison Street between Taylor and Lombard Avenues necessitated the removal of a block of homes, it was deemed that having the seat of local government in that location would signal the commitment to a community that was not prepared to write off a key section in the face of perceived racial change and business disinvestment. Originally, the logical choice of the block to be developed was between Lyman and Taylor, as it had smaller homes and more of them were in disrepair, but the existence of the abandoned Fencl Chevrolet dealership on Madison between Taylor and Lombard Avenues meant that choosing that location offered the additional opportunity to get rid of a major eyesore. In addition, as Lombard was a through street, running under both the Green Line tracks and across the Eisenhower, having access to that street was deemed valuable for the easy deployment of police cars.

By 1973, the prominent Chicago architect Harry Weese was commissioned to develop a design for a new village hall that would include almost all functions and house all of the major equipment other than that of the old fire station. The citizens whose two dozen homes were to be removed to make way for the building were generally satisfied with the financial offer of the village, and not much time was spent in what could have been a contentious struggle to assemble the property, even with the advantage of eminent domain. Residents of short standing were offered what they had paid for their homes, plus a bonus of $500 if they signed up within a designated time period.[114] The design was tweaked and accepted. Erected fairly expeditiously, the building was opened in 1975, and the old village hall was demolished. While the commitment of the village was important, equally so was that many of the people forced from their homes chose to relocate within the community.

Weese's design was not only modern instead of classical but also featured an open courtyard meant to house public events. The staff was separated from people there via only a low wooden counter, making the space inviting

Above: President James McClure cuts the ribbon at the dedication of the new village hall in 1975. Three of the six trustees stand by for the momentous move of the seat of village government to east Oak Park. *Courtesy of the Village of Oak Park.*

Below: This aerial view shows the entire village hall complex, from the east, in Harry Weese's design influenced by the Finnish architect Alvar Aalto. The council chambers are on the lower right of the courtyard. *Courtesy of the Village of Oak Park.*

and the staff accessible. Glass made up the entire inner walls facing the courtyard. Unfortunately, the realities of late twentieth century urban life meant that almost everyone who arrived at the village hall came by car and entered from the parking lot entrance. Thus, almost nobody since then comes up the hall's incline to and through the courtyard, and the space has seldom been used for public functions, which tend to take place in the parks closer to the center of the village.

Members of the village board in place when the new village hall was opened were some of the most activist and vocal citizens in support of programs that enhanced integration without resegregation. They wanted to increase participation in local government by residents in all demographic categories and felt that the tendency for people to remain on commissions for many terms helped create a sense of exclusivity. Under the presidency of James McClure, an informal but long-lasting policy of commissioners serving only two consecutive terms was established. A few years later, a Community Involvement Commission was created, with the express goal of finding more minority, women and renters to serve on the many village commissions, and it still serves that purpose.

Besides supporting the efforts of the Community Relations Commission and Department, the Housing Center and block clubs, in trying to maintain diversity, one of the trustees, Robert Varnes, championed an affirmative quota system in the part of the village that had already experienced the most integration. His plan received the support of almost half of the Community Relations Commission in 1974. Generally known as the "quota plan," the concept was discussed for the next several years, but many saw the plan as overtly racist and exclusionary and of dubious legal standing, thus it never received serious support from any village board. As one of the major fears in an integrating community was that real estate values would drop with blacks moving in, many people whose nearly entire financial stake was in their homes were the most frightened. Addressing that fear in 1977, the village board adopted an innovative Equity Assurance Program, which had been suggested by a local group of female activists, "First Tuesday." For the cost of an appraisal, one could buy into the program, with a guarantee from the village that it would pay the enrollee 80 percent of the difference between the appraised value of the home and the highest offer that failed to meet the appraised value. Fewer than two hundred people joined the program, and with real estate values climbing, nobody ever made a claim. The program, like many others, was just one—but a key—strategy to calm fears, give peaceful integration a chance and limit white flight.

On another front, the township government had been growing and adding a substantial number of services and new programs in the late 1960s and early 1970s, including mental health and youth services, Meals-at-Home and committees on senior issues, child care and community health. The institution had also survived a push to abolish the township form of government in Oak Park. The citizen who made the proposal cited the wastefulness of having coterminous taxing bodies and suggested that the duties of the township be transferred to the village government. The moderator at an annual meeting conceded the validity of many of the points made but "suggested that many special purpose taxing districts such as those for parks, mosquito abatement, and mental health be merged into the existing township structure."[115]

The proposal was defeated, and it was suggested that the issue be revisited in a decade. With all of the new programs and offices needed for staff and clients, the diverse rented facilities were inadequate and costly, so the township acquired its first permanent home, on South Oak Park Avenue, just south of the el stop and with its own small parking lot. The building was remodeled and the new programs consolidated in the new space. Additional services were added in the next few years, but the facility was inadequate to house them less than a decade after the move. The public elected township board candidates who supported the new and expanded programs and services, and with far less fanfare than what accompanied the construction of village hall, the township building was expanded.

The Township of Oak Park administration finally moved to its own home, at 105 South Oak Park Avenue, in 1975. The current expanded offices date to 1987. *Courtesy of Oak Park Township.*

Politically, the village and the township were operated very differently, with village board members elected after the start of the village manager system typically serving one term, and some two, but the township elected officials often stayed in office for much longer periods. There was no longer any overlap between the officers of both taxing bodies, as there had been in the early days after disconnection from Cicero Township, and efforts to work together on programs were only modest. With the advent of youth services, greater programmatic cooperation among the township, the village's youth officer, the high school and the parks and recreation programs came into being.

Economic development was the twin pillar with racial diversity, supporting the community in the minds of most citizens who chose to remain here and work for change. With the substantial expenditures being incurred on public works and the new village hall, at the same time that the car dealers were starting to leave and several of the major retail outlets were relocating or simply closing, the business community and the village board began seeking answers to shore up and expand the tax base.

The first key move in the direction of responding to the key question of how to generate economic development was the establishment of the Oak Park Development Corporation as a not-for-profit organization, with the mission of creating programs and incentives to bring new business to the community and help those already established to grow. The major banks, other organizations and the village became partners in working together to make sources of funding more easily available and, when possible, at lower rates. A local retired executive of a major company was the first executive director, and others followed. The OPDC Board also included several citizens from various walks of civic life, but the banking community provided the major leadership.

Not only was the tax base slowly eroding, but the largest and most dramatic impact was also seen and felt on Lake Street, between Harlem and Forest Avenues, the traditional "downtown" of Oak Park. As the branch stores of prominent retailers started to close, so did other smaller stores, resulting in vacancies and the remaining retail firms doing less business than even before the nearby malls had opened. As early as late 1969, the Lake/Marion merchants were asking the village board to create a separate district and remove the then existing parking requirements in that location. The board was open to the suggestions and referred the requests to appropriate commissions.[116] By 1971, the business community was touting the Oak Park Center Plan as a response to the Oak Brook, North Riverside and other area malls. The plan was to create a mall-like environment in downtown Oak Park, as it "is suggested as a method of making Lake-Marion-Harlem retailing more aggressive, increasing shopper convenience and loyalty to Oak Park stores, attracting high quality shoppers, goods retailers, and allowing the area to compete with planned shopping centers on a stronger footing."[117] Even utilizing or incorporating the site of the abandoned Lowell School was discussed by the village board in 1970 as part of a possible new business plan.

In response to the requests of the merchants for a separate taxing district and with visions of a new urban mall, the village came up with the idea of a special service taxing district, but in 1973 the Illinois Supreme Court ruled that such a practice would be illegal. The community response was similar to Oak Park's earlier attempts to control the sale of liquor and for separation from Cicero Township: friendly local legislators proposed and led the fight to pass legislation that would allow municipalities to institute a special tax program to finance downtown development projects. Oak Park's plan would be the test case of the new law's validity, as approved in 1974.[118] Much of the discussion revolved around the new mall having uniform hours, common

Heavy equipment is hard at work tearing up Lake Street as the first step in establishing the pedestrian mall in 1974. Many of the stores pictured were parts of national chains, and all have been replaced by other retail establishments and restaurants. *Courtesy of HSOPRF.*

advertising and promotions and various lease agreements, but achieving that kind of control or commitment was elusive—and not for the last time.

One major problem was that many, if not most, of the merchants who operated their businesses and supported the street closures were not the owners of the buildings housing their stores. Not surprisingly, the owners of those properties were strongly opposed to a taxation structure relating to the district without being able to pass on the taxes to the tenants holding long-term leases. An even more intractable problem surfaced when agreements involving uniform hours to attract shoppers and related matters were brought up for ratification. While most of the business owners agreed on the necessity for uniformity if they were to compete with the malls, many proprietors of mom and pop retail shops demurred, claiming that they were unable to put in the longer hours associated with five-day-a-week evening hours and couldn't afford to hire the staff needed to respond. Because they had long-term leases, there was really no way to force them to conform. Some threatened to leave the area if forced into such a schedule. The village hoped for the best but got no guarantees of cooperation from the merchants and instead moved ahead with the mall, which opened to acclaim in 1974, with great hopes for the future.

At the same time, in the 1970s, as the departure of traditional auto dealers along Madison Street was accelerating, another transportation issue came into play. An unexpected boost, in the form of a silver lining to a major economic cloud, came from the national gasoline shortage of 1973, resulting from the Mideast oil crisis. While almost everyone was affected throughout the country, and Oak Parkers were among those facing closed stations and long lines to get gasoline for the week, the local transportation system became a valuable asset in marketing the community. With two el lines and the commuter train all reaching the end of the village, and with bus routes serving the main north–south streets, Oak Parkers could get to work in downtown Chicago and many other locations without a hitch. Suddenly, and with the consequent rise in gas prices (and not for the last time), a home or apartment close to public transportation seemed like a good bet, and the village was not slow in touting that advantage.

The creation of the mall and the previously mentioned transportation issues were important, yet at the same time as the mall was opening, a seemingly modest plan to develop a farmers' market was hatched by two local boosters. Marge Gockel and Carla Lind were impressed with other farmers' markets they had seen and proposed such a venture to the village board. A commission was formed in 1975, planning was completed and the Oak Park

Left: The Oak Park Farmers' Market is a much beloved institution that attracts both Oak Parkers and people from Chicago and the surrounding suburbs. Not only do the farmers from neighboring states bring fresh produce, meat and flowers, but the music and donuts also have loyal followers. *Courtesy of the Village of Oak Park.*

Below: Gene Wulbert's Ford dealership was one of the many automobile showrooms/service facilities on "Automobile Row" on Madison Street. He advertised as the "Home of the Van King" and specialized in large, customized vans. Later, the building was used by two cable TV companies. *Courtesy of HSOPRF.*

Farmers' Market was opened on North Boulevard in the summer of 1976. With fruits, vegetables, plants, flowers and, later, live music and donuts made under the sponsorship of local not-for-profit organizations, the venture moved into the parking lot of Pilgrim Congregational Church in 1978. As the market grew and expanded, occasional skirmishes with neighbors and accusations of unfair competition from local merchants resulted, but its citizen commission and part-time staff were able to negotiate the issues. The market became a Saturday morning fixture, meeting place and destination for people from many surrounding communities. With little expense and the support of a strong volunteer base for the one day a week that it is open, the farmers' market became more able to serve as a community focal point than the mall was ever able to become.

Chapter 10

THE ALL-AMERICA CITY, THE EXCHANGE CONGRESS, HERITAGE TOURISM AND JUNIOR HIGH SCHOOLS

In 1975–76, Oak Park was one of the ten communities selected as an "All-America City" by the National Civic League, which cited three major accomplishments that earned the village the award: the Oak Park Housing Center, the Oak Park Mall and the Frank Lloyd Wright Home and Studio. Capitalizing on the award and the then concurrent American bicentennial for the utmost in public relations, the village launched a major marketing initiative with the cooperation and help of the organizations that had provided the impetus for the award. The village's Mall Commission hosted events, the Housing Center utilized the positive publicity of the award to further tout the community as a great place for people of diverse backgrounds to live and the village itself launched the first of a major event and initiative in the form of the Oak Park Exchange Congress in 1977.

The congress brought together elected officials, representatives of local organizations and activist citizens from the older, mostly collar suburbs around major cities from all over the United States. Dedicated to highlighting the accomplishments of Oak Park, comparing notes and networking with and learning from one another, the delegates were invited to stay in the homes of local residents, were given tours of the community, participated in panel discussions and heard various speakers. The twin issues of economic development and diversity dominated the first and subsequent exchange congresses, both in Oak Park and in other communities. Participants left energized by seeing that other communities faced similar issues and that there were approaches and programs available to be developed.

Oak Park Housing Center's founder Roberta Raymond and a then Community Relations Division staff member, Sandra Sokol, review the list of delegates to the 1988 Oak Park Exchange Congress in the lobby of village hall. *Courtesy of HSOPRF.*

Among the activities at the first exchange congress was to have delegates visit the Frank Lloyd Wright Home and Studio, one of the three legs on which the All-America city nomination had been based, and to see the other Wright architecture in Oak Park. The F.L. Wright Home and Studio Foundation had been founded in 1974, with the express aim of acquiring and restoring the Wright property to its original condition. With the help of local lending organizations and the Oak Park Development Corporation realizing the home and studio's potential as a tourist attraction, the building became the first co-stewardship property of the National Trust for Historic Preservation but was restored and run by a local board. By the time of the first exchange congress, the building had become listed as a national landmark on the National Register of Historic Places in 1976, joining Wright's Unity Temple (designated in 1971) as the second national landmark in Oak Park. Architectural tourism was then on its way to becoming a vital part of both the economic and the social currency of the community.

There had been a great deal written about Frank Lloyd Wright and his architecture over the years, and the impressive Unity Temple had long been a place of pilgrimage for visitors from around the world. Yet visitorship

The first village celebration of Frank Lloyd Wright and his architecture took place on the presumed 100th anniversary of his birth in 1969. These stamps were issued to commemorate the occasion and mark the start of heritage tourism in Oak Park. *Courtesy of HSOPRF.*

had always been personal and mostly individual—except for an occasional professor of architecture or architectural historian taking students on a field trip. Thus, both the impact and the identification with Oak Park, per se, were minimal.

The first major attempt to take a look at the work and bring people to the community took place in 1969 (the supposed centennial of Wright's birth), when a group of local architects, supporters and faculty from University of Illinois at Chicago mounted a Wright festival and published a guide to his architecture in Oak Park and River Forest. That event had the effect of drawing more attention to the rich architectural heritage of the area and helped focus the community on the problematic ownership of both Unity Temple as a living church and the Wright Home and Studio in private hands. The modest guide published for the event was republished as an introduction to Wright's architecture in the area, appearing under the auspices of the local chamber of commerce. Unity Temple Restoration Foundation was established to restore and preserve the landmark building in 1973, and the Wright Home and Studio Foundation was next in 1974. At least $3 million was raised and spent on the restoration of the home and studio, and the success of those efforts in increasing tourism led to the creation of the Tour Center under the jurisdiction of the Wright Home and Studio. Another focal point of emerging tourism was the Wright Plus annual walk. Wright Plus continues to attract people from around the world, and the 2011 walk will be the thirty-seventh consecutive event. Later the Tourism Bureau became a freestanding organization, and heritage tourism was born as an industry in Oak Park.

Also as a result of the new awareness of the impact of historic preservation on a community, Oak Park not only established its first of three historic

The Frank Lloyd Wright Home and Studio had long attracted architectural enthusiasts when it was purchased and became a National Trust co-steward property in 1974. The Frank Lloyd Wright Preservation Trust now administers both the home and studio and Wright's Robie House in Chicago. *Courtesy of the author.*

districts but was also awarded certified local government status for its Historic Preservation Commission in 1994. In addition, the village also sponsored the publication of guidebooks to the Wright and Ridgeland historic districts, further increasing awareness of the architectural treasures and richness of the community. To help ensure the permanence of the buildings within their boundaries, coterminous local districts were approved by the village board, adding a level of protection not provided by the listing on the National Register of Historic Places. The Historic Preservation Commission also conducted periodic surveys of the architecture of the community, mounted photographic exhibitions and made suggestions for adjustments to the boundaries of the districts in the light of new research.

Yet a great many old homes and apartment buildings were demolished and replaced by larger apartment buildings and condos in the 1960s and 1970s without much opposition. As the replacement structures were generally well built (though lacking in architectural distinction) and had to provide a minimum of one parking space per unit, they were greeted with guarded

Marion Garden Condominiums is an elegant contemporary in design elevator building, built for condominiums 13 years ago. Exceptionally spacious apartments in choice location offer comfortable living and sound investment.

Lobby

Transportation
- 2 blocks to Lake St. "L" and Northwestern R.R.
- 5 min. to Eisenhower Expressway
- 1 block to Shopping Mall

Construction- steel- masonry- concrete
- Stone and brick exterior
- Plastered walls
- Poured concrete floors
- Garage and outside parking
- All electric building
- Elevator

Apartments
- 8- 3 bedrooms-2 baths- 2 parking spaces
- 2300 to 2400 sq. ft.
- 32- 2 bedrooms- 1½ baths- 1 parking space
- 1100 to 1400 sq. ft.

Special Features
- Recreation room
- Newly decorated hallways
- Available additional parking

Lobby
- Newly decorated lobby
- Terrazzo floor and "Travertine" marble walls

During the 1960s, there was a wave of apartment building, differing from those of the 1920s in having parking and elevators. Some were built as condominiums, and others were converted in the 1970s. This brochure is typical in its depiction of amenities, convenience and quality. *Courtesy of the author.*

approval. As the condo buildings usually replaced smaller structures and sold for more, the twin effects on the tax base and the always difficult parking situation were salutary.

Starting in 1972, the Community Design Commission also contributed to the awareness of and pride in the village's housing stock by presenting annual Cavalcade of Pride awards to the owners of homes (and businesses) in recognition of the exemplary restoration or maintenance of their properties. And though not all of the winners of that award have performed historically accurate restoration, the results have included the recognition of the owners of the buildings, setting an example for neighbors and creating a major ripple effect throughout the community. A Frank Lloyd Wright Annual Race was even initiated in 1976, with the park district sponsoring the event as much to capitalize on the newfound fame of the architect as to promote fitness.

The success of the Wright Prairie School District not only attracted more attention to historic preservation but also created additional tensions between the residential community and the institutions within. When a Ridgeland Historic District was first proposed in the late 1970s, the opposition to

The former First Church of Christ, Scientist, is now the Arts Center of Oak Park and houses the Hemingway Museum on the ground floor, south on Oak Park from the Hemingway Birthplace Home. *Courtesy of Ernest Hemingway Foundation of Oak Park.*

including West Suburban Hospital within the district was sufficient to cause trustees who wanted to incorporate the hospital's buildings within the district to vote with those who wanted to derail the district. A later village board approved the district, including the hospital.

A decade after the formation of the Wright Home and Studio Foundation, the Ernest Hemingway Foundation was founded and a museum opened near his birthplace. That home was purchased in 1992 and opened to the public the following year. Fundraising and pro bono work by local advocates helped ensure a faithful restoration, and the Hemingway Boyhood Home was acquired later for future development. As with the Wright attractions, scholarship, education and increasing public awareness became part of the foundation's mission, with lectures, symposia and special tours arranged to broaden the impact beyond the aficionados to a larger public.

Other independent Oak Park organizations, three of which are part of the park district, have also contributed to the development of tourism and increased public awareness of Oak Park. The Oak Park Conservatory had been started in 1914 as a collection of exotic plants brought back by travelers, and the present glass greenhouse dates from 1929.[119] Having fallen into disrepair and threatened with demolition in the late 1960s, a grass-roots group that became the Friends of the Oak Park Conservatory was organized by local activist Elsie Jacobson and raised funds to ensure the repair and maintenance of the building. Much later, a community room was added to run workshops and related activities. Still owned and operated by the park district, the conservatory is open to the public at no charge.

The John Farson mansion, later owned by the Mills family, had been acquired by the park district, with the historical society occupying the upper floors since 1970. Another preservation organization, the Pleasant Home Foundation, was founded in 1990 to preserve and restore the Farson-Mills Home, with the new name reflecting its location at the corner of Pleasant and Home Avenues. This building became another national landmark in 1999, and its own foundation sponsors tours and lectures and supports its restoration. Another large home that was adapted to public use was designed by Charles White in 1913. It is now known as the Cheney mansion and consists of the home, a coach house and a greenhouse. Deeded to the park district in 1975, it became open to the public upon the death of the donor, Elizabeth Cheney. It, too, is open for tours and various community purposes.

The two Wright-associated organizations and the Hemingway foundations, plus the volunteers at the three park district properties, among them have about 600 people giving tours, working at these venues' gift shops and helping serve the 100,000 people who visit Oak Park each year as heritage tourists. A new direction in economic development was taken with the support of the organizations themselves, the tourism board and elected officials. The board of realtors became enthusiastic and submitted a plan, in 1973, to rename North Boulevard after Frank Lloyd Wright and South Boulevard after Ernest Hemingway. The suggestion was never acted on, but the point was that tourism was being taken seriously as a real estate marketing tool.

The growth of the tourism industry was even more important for its psychological and public relations effects than for the tourism dollars attracted to event and institution admissions, restaurants and other retail establishments, bringing more people to the community who then found it an attractive and desirable place to live. Similarly, the founding of the Oak Park Festival Theatre in 1975, originally showing one Shakespeare play per year, not only provided high-quality entertainment for local residents but also drew visitors from around the Chicago area. The first play was performed on Westgate, but the venue was soon changed to nearby Austin Gardens, where the summer productions continue to this day. The tourism board members and local restaurants also tried to capitalize on that added constituency. And soon they were helped by a change in longtime policy and the very image of the village.

The boost to both tourism and the tax base in general was the momentous decision to reverse one hundred years of Oak Park as a dry community and to allow liquor licenses for full-service restaurants. The restaurant base had always been minimal in Oak Park, with some fast-food restaurants and scattered coffee shops. With the first liquor licenses going in 1979 to La Majada Mexican restaurant and the decidedly upscale Philander's, everything was about to change. All kinds of restaurants began to open, though there were challenges to what kind of bar could be part of an establishment and whether patrons were actually just visiting the bar and then leaving without eating. That issue, which was never really clarified nor policed, involved restrictions that required patrons ordering alcoholic beverages to order food as well. However, the attempt to bring quality restaurants to the village while continuing to keep out traditional neighborhood bars worked. While it has proved difficult to quantify the impact on tourism and tourist dollars, the availability of good restaurants of all types certainly helped the economy and filled some of the empty stores along the major business streets.

As the exchange congress was trying to convey to the world, diverse communities are not to be feared and avoided, and they should capitalize on all of their assets. Heritage tourism brought and continues to bring

The Oak Park Festival Theatre started out doing Shakespeare but later added other classics and, recently, the plays of contemporary writers. Many well-known Chicago actors have graced the stage in Austin Gardens, here with a performance of *Doctor Faustus* starring Francis Guinan as Faust. *Courtesy of Oak Park Festival Theater.*

thousands of people to look around Oak Park, and many decided that it was a wonderful place to visit and perhaps live. As a writer talking about how history and culture could serve as meaningful economic development tools noted in the *Wall Street Journal* in 1976, "The Historic District and the tours helped Oak Park by drawing attention to its treasures."[120] The bed-and-breakfast inn became another kind of business developed to capitalize

After more than a century as a legally "dry" community, the first liquor licenses were issued in 1979, limited to full-service restaurants. Philander's was named after the amateur photographer whose images graced the establishment. *Courtesy of Carleton of Oak Park.*

on the new tourist industry. The first, Toad Hall, opened in 1987, and Under the Ginkgo Tree (still in business in 2010) came soon after, offering visitors a chance to stay in beautifully restored and upgraded Victorian homes.

The Oak Park Exchange Congresses lasted from 1977 through 1994, with the event held in alternate years in Oak Park and other communities after 1978. A regional congress took place in 2000, but the combination of successes, new leadership in many communities and the drain on volunteer time all contributed to its demise. On the more positive side, the many lessons learned and many program initiatives internalized by local governments may have made the congresses no longer necessary. Another legacy of the exchange congresses was the stronger awareness generated among local elected officials of the potential of cooperating on programs as diverse as shared dispatch of public safety officers, grants in support of redevelopment and other significant activities, often with neighboring towns.

For all of the success of the congresses and the effort put into facing the problems head-on, the two most intractable issues remained: economic and racial diversity. The creation of the Oak Park Mall represented a major attempt to deal with the deteriorating economic base. At the same time, changes in the structure of the elementary school district served as the primary response to the pattern of racial change in the community. Both were pioneering and untried reactions to concrete problems, and each had its share of both supporters and detractors. The tax burden on building owners and the difficulty of getting cooperation from retail merchants were noted but not addressed, and the mall was born. However, the problem of addressing racial imbalance in the schools affected all taxpaying citizens and had a day-to-day impact on all families with children enrolled in the schools in Elementary School District 97.

We have seen that there had been a push for implementing a junior high school system in the early 1960s but that public opinion favored maintaining the ten neighborhood schools that ran from kindergarten through the eighth grade. Several different issues faced the community when the school restructuring issue resurfaced almost a decade later. In addition to the slow but real growth of the African American population affecting racial balance issues, the expanding demographic of working mothers had made lunch at school more appealing for all grade levels while lessening the importance of children returning home for lunch. With the same working mothers looking for after school child care, a couple of Hawthorne School parents identified with the school's Community Council developed a program for Hephzibah Home to provide such care at the same time that a place was found for children to eat lunch at school. Introduced in the mid-1970s, those programs soon spread throughout the district.

A referendum to increase school funding had passed by a two-to-one margin in 1972, and the district began to examine racial balance in a policy statement of 1974. A newly created Committee for Tomorrow's Schools brought back a set of suggested choices in December of that year: develop special interest centers, start a voluntary transfer plan, create junior high schools or develop middle schools. The choices were narrowed to the last two options, and the end of K-8 was inevitable. Candidates for integration plan were elected to the open school board positions in the spring of 1975, and with Hawthorne and Longfellow schools out of compliance with state guidelines on racial balance in the schools in a district, a unanimous board voted for a two-junior-high-school plan with busing in January 1976. As a clear indication and show of support for quality schools of whatever structure, the citizens of Oak Park voted in support of both the elementary and the high school districts by approving referenda for both in December 1976. Yet less than ten years later, the topic of school consolidation was back on the table. Legislation proposed at the state level would have enabled communities to opt for unit districts, rather than maintaining separate school boards for the elementary and high schools. The issue was hotly debated but died for lack of a state mandate.[121]

With heritage tourism established, the new mall in place, a completely reorganized and popularly funded elementary school district and a high school district flush with voter approval via referendum, the first exchange congress had much to offer other communities that faced similar challenges with far less support. For at least a while, the voters were in support of change and adaptation, the taxing bodies and the private sector had formed new partnerships and the All-America city looked to the future.

Chapter 11

CHALLENGES FROM WITHIN AND WITHOUT

N ot long after the first exchange congress took place, a series of widely diverse issues had an impact on how the village both perceived itself and was seen by the outside world. On January 13, 1979, the Chicago area experienced the second-heaviest snowfall in its recorded history, and the snow was compounded by additional amounts the next day. The entire area was affected, but Oak Park had a somewhat different problem because of its use of alleys and parking ban on village streets. Elected officials and staff produced an unusual plan to plow the alleys first so that cars could be removed from both the arterial and side streets. For those whose cars had nowhere to go (often because of collapsed garages), the next emergency step was to institute temporary parking (alternate side of the street) as an aid to snow removal. Some of the results of that emergency were to have an effect on future snow removal plans.

A different kind of storm hit the following year when the American Nazi Party appeared before the village board requesting a permit to march on a Saturday in 1980. The board, comprising Catholic, Jewish and Protestant members, voted unanimously to allow the parade, letting the village president express their abhorrence of all that the Nazis stood for but reiterating the democratic right of all to demonstrate. President James McClure also urged all citizens to stay away and ignore the event rather than give the group the publicity it was seeking. The parade went on as scheduled, with only thirteen party members appearing and the police removing any signs that could be used as weapons.[122] Counterdemonstrators included members from various

When the American Nazi Party asked for a permit to march in Oak Park in 1980, the board of trustees unanimously approved the following week as the time for the event, to provide minimal opportunity to the hate group to generate publicity. *Courtesy of HSOPRF.*

groups outside the village, thereby keeping much of the confrontation between two outside groups. The onlookers shouted down the speakers, and the police moved the group out when the allotted time was over. Oak Parkers who wished to show their opposition participated in a vigil at Unity Temple. There had been no visible local support for the Nazi march, but that was not the case when a different kind of Nazi-related issue surfaced only three years later.

Reinholdt Kulle, a janitor at Oak Park and River Forest High School, stood accused of having lied on his application to enter the United States in the 1950s by not revealing his role as a guard at a wartime concentration camp and as a member of the Waffen SS. Kulle eventually admitted that he had served as a guard but claimed a "soldier's defense," averring that he not only had not committed any atrocities but also had no knowledge of the activities that occurred within the facility. While the immigration authorities were investigating Kulle's case and the District 200 administration and board were debating whether his prior activities had any bearing on his employment, the public took strong positions on both sides of the issue.

That he had been an efficient and even helpful employee was argued by his supporters as grounds to retain him. Supporters also noted that Kulle had claimed to have not participated in atrocities, that the issue was past and that it was the decent thing to do to forgive. The opposing side opined that no amount of time erased what had been done and pointed out that a large difference existed between being a drafted soldier and a volunteer member of the Waffen SS and that it was beyond belief that he could not have known what was happening inside Gross-Rosen Concentration Camp while stationed there. Neighbors turned against neighbors, and longtime friendships were broken as Kulle's supporters within and outside the school started a defense fund for him. The high school board met and decided to put Kulle on paid leave in January 1984, noting that he would not be rehired when his (verbal) contract expired in June of that year. The Immigration Service found that he had lied, and he was later deported.[123]

Another contentious issue that, like the Nazi march, was part of a larger societal issue was the local participation in the attempt to have Nestlé Company stop marketing infant formula to mothers in impoverished countries with unsanitary water supplies. Critics based their claim on the grounds that mother's milk was safer (and more affordable) than formula mixed with unsanitary water. The focal point of the issue was the projected opening of a restaurant of the Nestlé subsidiary, Stouffer's, called the Cheese Cellar, at the highly visible corner of Oak Park Avenue and Lake Street.

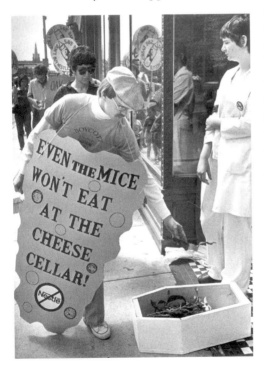

The boycott of the Cheese Cellar restaurant was directed at parent company Nestlé's marketing of infant formula to African woman, who often had to mix the formula with unsafe water. Economic development was pitted against political activism in support of social causes. *Courtesy of HSOPRF.*

Again local citizens took two sides, with the protesters claiming that they were taking the only morally correct position in trying to affect public opinion and influence Nestlé to change its marketing policy and strategy. Others, including the liquor commission and the unanimous village board, claimed that the request for a local liquor license had nothing to do with its parent organization's activities in foreign countries. Also, the need for the economic stimulation to be gained from opening such an establishment was an important consideration in granting the liquor and business licenses in support of the restaurant. The local press was filled with both impassioned letters supporting the boycott and others that dismissed the protesters as naïve, misguided and/or radical, with family members often on opposing sides of the issue. The business was opened and was successful, but the protesters were also vindicated when Nestlé eventually made substantial policy changes. Later, the Cheese Cellar became Winberie's and remains the successful anchor of that corner location.

Less dramatically, several important changes occurred in the political arena, with the village board firing a village manager in 1980 for the first time in the VMA era. The succeeding manager developed a sophisticated management study that forced the police chief and a deputy into unexpected retirement just before the release of the study, which was critical of management of the police force. The election of 1981 pitted two former VMA endorsed trustees against each other for the presidency, with Sara Bode, the former director of the Oak Park Mall, endorsed by the VMA caucus and elected as the first female president of the village. In the same landmark election, Percy Slaughter was also elected as the first black trustee. There was much to be proud of in the diversity of the board, but the nature of the VMA slating process remained under attack as elitist and undemocratic.

Another change from the status quo was the 1980 founding of the *Wednesday Journal* as a serious and ongoing alternative to the *Oak Leaves*. Other newspapers had come and gone in the twentieth century, but none had ever challenged the long-established paper of record effectively or was sufficiently different in its point of view to attract a regular readership. From that point on, Oak Park was a two-newspaper town.

The previous board of trustees had effectively eliminated the sale of handguns in Oak Park, though the issue had created much passion and anger. Certain pro-gun activists contacted trustees and warned of rape and worse being perpetrated by people from Chicago if they lost the protection of their guns.[124] In 1984, another board went further, enacting an ordinance severely regulating the ownership of handguns by private individuals. A combination of local crimes, including four murders in 1983 in Oak Park and a major case of an Oak Parker killed in Chicago, led to strong advocacy for a gun ban, but substantial and vocal opposition arose as well.

A group called the Freedom Committee called for an advisory referendum for November 1985, and when it was held, the pro-ban side won by about two thousand votes. There were occasional tests of the ordinance when individuals were arrested for having guns in their possession and had used them in connection with stopping some sort of criminal activity at their homes. However, the issue was usually sidestepped, and charges were either not filed or were later dropped. Given the circumstances under which exceptions were made, many citizens deemed the issue to be as symbolic as the village being declared a nuclear freeze zone.

Less volatile issues included an examination of the needs of senior citizens, a matter first noted by the township in 1967 and addressed by the first Senior Citizens Committee formed by the township in 1971. The Meals-at-Home program was started that year, and in the following decade, senior transportation, information, energy, income tax preparation and nutrition services were offered for seniors as well. With the growth of a graying population in the community, the township also organized a senior lunch program and an activity center for that part of the citizenry.

While all of these services gained general support without any real suggestion of an alternative source, the feeling that the township was really an unnecessary part of government persisted. Yet, as in 1970, when dissolving the township had been discussed and voted down, its officials were fighting the accusation, this time as raised in the press. Twenty years later, in response to an editorial, the township supervisor wrote a spirited and detailed defense of the programs of the township government, with statistics on the number of meals served, bus rides provided, responses to requests for energy assistance and even investigations of cases of elder abuse.[125]

Also in regard to the rising percentage of senior citizens living in the village, and along with an increased sensitivity to the housing problems facing seniors and others with disabilities, both the public and the private sector started paying serious attention to housing issues affecting those groups. The Oak Park Arms, a longtime facility for extended occupancy, had already become a senior residence when the Housing Authority developed Mills Park Tower in 1975. Later, in 1980, the Oak Park Residence Corporation rehabilitated and converted a former dilapidated hotel on the village's east end into a seventy-unit subsidized rental property called the Oaks, for seniors and disabled persons, with priority given to those already residing in Oak Park. The Oaks also included congregate dining in its early years. Later, the Residence Corporation took the lead in adding the Ryan Farrelly Apartments, especially for people with severe physical disabilities but otherwise able to live on their own. The private sector responded, too, and Heritage House was opened in 1979 to serve the senior population as long as the residents were deemed qualified by HUD. Holley Court Terrace

An alternative to the older residential hotels and the buildings for seniors built by the Housing Authority or not-for-profit organizations is rental senior housing with many amenities at Holley Court Terrace. There are large public rooms, a restaurant with views of Chicago and limousine service for the tenants. *Courtesy of the author.*

was opened for seniors in 1987, but as a nonsubsidized facility, with limo service, handsome facilities and a thirteenth-floor terrace with scenic views of Chicago. More recently, Belmont Village, on Madison Street and next to Oak Park Hospital, has become another option for seniors.

In addition to the work of the township, a large number of private organizations in Oak Park had been devoted to the care of children and the economically disadvantaged for as long as a century, with the Associated Charities of Oak Park and Vicinity founded in 1891. But more specific needs were reflected in the 1972 referendum and push for a mental health center and change of the name of an old organization to Family Services and Mental Health Center. In 1990, the building that arose from the ashes of the long-vacant Lamar Theater received financial support from the family of native son and McDonald's chief Ray Kroc and was named after him. It also received public support, with Oak Parker Phillip Rock's assistance. In that regard, Rock, Illinois Senate president from 1979 to 1993, like Senator Henry Austin Jr. before him, was of tremendous help to the community. Addressing all kinds of family needs, the organization is now known as the Thrive Counseling Center.

Another response to human needs was the founding of Sarah's Inn as a not-for-profit organization in 1981. Recognizing that domestic violence, unsafe environments for women and children and more subtle forms of abuse were being missed by mainstream organizations and not confined to the less financially well-off, the new organization quickly came to provide many services, such as safe homes, emergency shelters, a hot line, child care and support services. And although the geographical range of the organization's activities spread to Chicago and many neighboring suburbs, Oak Park has remained its headquarters and a major source of the funds raised to carry out its mission.

Perhaps because it was time for a change after all of the stress of dealing with the hot issues, or perhaps because of other forces at work, the village board election of 1985 was a tradition breaker in that three seats were won by a non-VMA-backed slate campaigning under the banner CARE. The CARE candidates included the founder of the Neighborhood Watch program, Susan Helfer; she and her colleagues had run for office because they believed that the village board had lost direction. In this case, however, the board turned out not as divided as the election results suggested, as Patricia Andrews, one of the three CARE candidates, broke with her organization and tended to vote with the VMA majority. Clouding the issue of whether the results reflected only policy issues was the fact that one of the three VMA-backed candidates who lost was a black man and two others were Jews, raising at least the possibility that prejudice was behind the results, especially as over the next couple of decades, many of the VMA candidates who lost in contested elections were members of racial or religious minority groups.

A major change in the structure of election to the village board was the board's 1989 decision, without referendum, to change from the election of all members of the board at the same time to staggered terms. Surprisingly little public debate or specific objection resulted, with only two former trustees testifying against the change. However, many in the community came to regret the need for political campaigns every two years. Two years later, three slates competed for three positions, with elections to four positions in subsequent two-year cycles, and multiple slates often vied for the board positions in the following years.

The year 1985 was the completion date of the fourteen-year gestation of Forest Place, an extensive residential project that eventually included a fifteen-story tower and a large group of town homes. Its origins were in 1971, when developer Jonas Stankus bought the property of the former

Lowell School and District 97 headquarters and requested permission to build two fifty-four-story towers. Denied such a variance in zoning, he scaled back several times and finally planned a thirty-five-story building to be federally subsidized. Irate neighbors demanded that the HUD backing sought by Stankus necessitated an environmental impact study because of the site's proximity to historic district buildings and the "shadow cast on Unity Temple," a national landmark. Stankus sued but lost in 1977. After HUD withdrew its support, the village bought the property for roughly the same price as Stankus had paid and then sold it to a new developer. The project as finally built was approved in 1984 and constructed over the next two years, with the village guaranteeing a $16.5 million industrial revenue bond.[126] This project can be considered the grandfather of village involvement in shared economic development programs for the next several decades, though it was one of the most divisive issues in the community. Only the question of using tax incremental financing for downtown development, and the impact on the other local taxing bodies, caused as much discussion in the economic arena.

In addition to the issues of high-rise developments and public financial participation in these projects, it soon became clear that the mall was not helping downtown Oak Park flourish as a shopping destination. The

Twelve years after developer Jonas Stankus bought the old Lowell School site, construction on Forest Place was finally initiated. The town homes were developed first, followed by the fifteen-story rental apartment building. *Courtesy of HSOPRF.*

Lake Theater was suffering, too, from being a one-screen operation, and the owners did a major renovation, turning the interior into three smaller theaters in 1984 and adding a fourth the next year while rehabbing the exterior and maintaining the Art Deco look. A decade later, three more theaters were added behind the neighboring storefronts, creating a more competitive seven theaters while preserving the old downtown look.

Various plans for the rest of the shopping area were proposed, but nothing came of them, including the suggestion that the conversion of retail space to second-floor offices that had proved successful in several of the buildings on Lake Street might become a model for the whole area.[127] However, this turned out to be an impractical idea, especially as many of the most underutilized buildings had no elevators to upper floors.

Within a decade of the mall's creation, both merchants and the village government began discussions about tearing it out, at least along the Lake Street corridor. Too many complaints from businesses that nobody knew they were there and other gripes convinced the authorities that the mall had to go. Again, citizens protested, but this time not just about saving the beloved mall. The Committee to Save the Mall filed suit, charging that removal of the mall would be expensive and involve TIF (Tax Incremental Financing) suing because the expensive plan would use TIF monies for what the group deemed an inappropriate use. The committee got a restraining order from a judge in 1988 and had more than five thousand names on petitions. However, the other taxing bodies refused to join the suit, and the opposition disbanded after the restraining order wasn't renewed. The one concession to public opinion (as well as the reality of the cost) was that Marion Street and Westgate remained as a closed mall. Tied to the reopening of Lake Street was the same old issue described in the *Chicago Tribune* as "centralized management of the district, including uniform leasing rules, design elements and hours."[128] Just as when the mall was created, the merchants who demanded the expensive and ambitious plan would not agree to any standard pact or rules of management, and the village government again capitulated.

At the same time as Lake Street issues were debated, several strip malls were established, as many developers felt that they were the only way to utilize the shallow parcels of land along North, Lake, Madison and Chicago Avenues. Neighborhood residents didn't want these retail strips in their backyards, especially given that many contained fast food and convenience stores, but at least they provided parking for their patrons, keeping them off the side streets. These strip malls were easier to manage,

This strip mall on North and Harlem Avenues is characteristic of those built in the 1980s and 1990s: one story tall, with parking in front and with standardized façades. The number of bays in a given store distinguishes its design from its neighbors. *Courtesy of the author.*

had the parking and were only one story. However, turnover was and remains high, and the businesses located in strip malls have typically shown the same pattern, with convenience stores, dry cleaners, self-service laundromats and takeout food stores predominating. One of the Madison Street strip malls even housed a liquor store for a while, but that business, like two others operating as upscale wine merchants, failed to compete successfully with the large chains and closed.

One very controversial presence was that of storefront religious facilities, located both in some strip malls and former retail spaces. Several congregations became occupants, often over the objection of both the residential citizenry and neighboring merchants who wanted retail to support retail. The first such congregation was on Madison Street, where both the church and administrative offices were located side by side. Later, the congregation moved to a large facility in the adjacent suburb of Forest Park. After another religious center stirred controversy by locating on South Boulevard, the Fellowship Christian Church took over a funeral home on Madison Street, near the west end of town, raising the same issues of zoning, religious freedom and fears of racial change.

Perhaps class was an issue at least as important as race in regard to these congregations, as blacks and whites worshiped together in many of Oak Park's large mainstream churches, with several having highly regarded black clergy and lay leaders. It was the storefront, along with its association with poor black neighborhoods, that frightened white Oak Parkers. At the same time, there was no serious public outcry when a black congregation moved into a vacant existing church at Austin and Washington Boulevards. Slowly did the community adjust to these forces of change. Later, a Zen Center, a Buddhist Center, an orthodox Jewish Chabad and Orthodox Christian and Baha'i congregations also moved into nontraditional spaces in the village. Nonetheless, class remained a source of conflict within the community and even within individuals, as the desire for encouraging diversity clashed with established norms of decorum and lifestyle.

A more complicated and divisive controversy developed when the First Church of Christ, Scientist, decided, after seventy years, to move to smaller quarters in 1987 and sell its large and elegant building on Oak Park Avenue. Among the bidders was a black congregation from the West Side of Chicago, which made a substantial offer, contingent on getting a needed mortgage. The Oak Park Development Corporation countered with an offer but withdrew when strong allegations were made that it wanted to purchase the building only to keep out the black congregation. The seller then solicited sealed bids and accepted an offer from the owner of many buildings in town, Chatka Ruggiero. Her only contingency was the easing of zoning requirements for parking to enable the building's use as the Arts Center of Oak Park. After the building was purchased and adapted for that purpose, the Hemingway Museum took over space on the lower floor in 1991.

Even before the creation of the arts center, there had been a call for the community to develop a publicly owned building to house the performing and fine arts. When the Cheney mansion came into the hands of the park district, and various other buildings came on the market, arts supporters tried to make the case for the financial benefits that would accrue to the community by having a building that various arts organizations could utilize and for which they would pay rent. Perennial stumbling blocks included the cost of erecting and outfitting such a building and how the groups wanted it built with public dollars. Such a push was made when the West Towns Company decided to leave Oak Park in 1983. A group of arts supporters proposed that the company's bus barn be converted into an arts center. The village president and several trustees were initially supportive, but the village planner and economic development interests opposed such a use and cost, and the buildings were demolished to make way for a Dominick's grocery.

Race continued to be an issue in the community, though often with the leadership making symbolic but important gestures toward recognizing diversity. In 1985, for example, Hawthorne Junior High School was renamed for Percy Julian. The next year, a local black physician, Gerald Clay, founded African American Parents for Purposeful Leadership (APPLE) to build support for the community's black youth, first at the high school and later in District 97 as well. Mentoring, tutoring and programs to help promote youth achievement made up the agenda, and award dinners were started in 1991. Internal politics and leadership issues emerged in the mid-1990s, but the organization regrouped and returned to the high school in 1996. There, while the students repeatedly voted to keep to the long tradition of having males wear suits and females wear white dresses to commencement, the change in the racial makeup of the graduating class was pronounced.

A major step toward having youth work cooperatively was the founding of the CAST and BRAVO theater programs at the junior high schools in the 1980s, with the hope that the programs would "foster good relationships among students of diverse backgrounds."[129] The selection of Oak Parker Marjorie Vincent as Miss Illinois in 1990 and then as Miss America in 1991 enhanced the pride of African Americans and others in the community. Also impressive, Monroe Saffold, a black Oak Park resident, won the Mr.

The graduating seniors at Oak Park and River Forest High School have followed traditions with few modifications in more than one hundred years. The women now can wear white pants, and the men wear suits instead of the cutaway tuxedos and formal vests of earlier days. *Courtesy of HSOPRF.*

America Body Building Competition in his class of competitors over forty and over six feet in 1990. Saffold later became a minister working at First Baptist Church of Oak Park.

The community was becoming more diverse beyond religion and race, as the Oak Park Area Lesbian and Gay Association was founded in 1989 with support that extended beyond its growing numbers of members. OPALGA members participated in gay pride events in Chicago, with their own floats, and urged greater member involvement and participation in civic life. The village responded in an official way, too, adding sexual orientation to the long-established "Diversity Statement" that each newly elected board adopted. Later, a predominantly gay and lesbian congregation, New Spirit Metropolitan Church, was formed, though many people of minority gender status had become congregants in Oak Park's increasingly accepting and welcoming churches and synagogues. In 1997, Joanne Trapani was elected to the board as the first openly "out" trustee and was elected president of the village in 2003, serving with another openly gay board member. VMA candidates supported the establishment of a domestic registry to help same-sex couples' lives, and the board passed an enabling ordinance in September

While the support of many worthy causes are important parts of the Community of Congregations activities, the annual interfaith Thanksgiving Service brings together people to learn each other's traditions. The 2007 service depicted was at First United Methodist Church. *Courtesy of Reverend Edgar Hiestand, for the COC.*

1997. The community as a whole was more accepting in many ways, as the village election of 1999 included two VMA black candidates who ran unopposed. Yet when no black trustee sat on the following board, some claimed that the election showed prejudice. Clearly, color still counted.

However, battle lines other than race were drawn, and many fundamentalist Christians were hostile toward participating in any activities with religious bodies that accepted gay and lesbian members and to liberal religious groups in general. When the Council of Churches morphed into the Community of Congregations in 1992, welcoming Unitarians, Jews, Muslims and others, the most conservative groups declined to join, though some of their individual members might choose to participate in such COC programs as PADS, the Food Pantry and Interfaith Thanksgiving service. By that time, Austin Boulevard Christian Church was a smaller congregation than it had been in years past, and it started renting space to a Muslim group. By 2007, there was an India Mission Teluga Methodist Church, a Chinese Bible Church, the St. John United Methodist Church (with its large group of worshipers of Philippine descent) and a Peace Center organized by Quakers, among others. The religious institutions of Oak Park were diverse in regard to race, color and ethnicity, as well as in almost every way imaginable.

The Oak Park schools also reflected the diversity of the community, but concern was growing that the junior high school model was not working. So, just like the village board rethought the mall, the District 97 Board reexamined the schools and decided to change the system again. In 1968, a board committee had suggested remodeling Whittier School and constructing two middle schools as part of its deliberations about overcrowding, but a move in that direction had been rejected. Then, in 1999, the voters approved a referendum that called for the demolition of Julian and Emerson Junior High Schools, building larger middle schools on the sites and renovating all of the elementary schools to reflect the new configuration. Improved science labs, computer facilities and physical education programs were among the issues. Although the winning bids for demolition and new construction produced a huge cost increase of $12 million, the project went ahead, coming in "on time and under budget" and enabling the new schools to open in the fall of 2002.[130]

While a large minority of the population thought the middle schools to be a band-aid for the real problems of education, several other issues in the schools aroused more passion and again involved issues of race. The first was the removal of murals at Hatch School that included stereotypes of Africans on a world map painted by a physically handicapped woman as part of a Works

When the decision was made to develop a middle school program, the two junior high schools were demolished, and large, fully equipped middle schools replaced them. Percy Julian and Gwendolyn Brooks Middle Schools are each named after important African American figures. *Courtesy of the author.*

Progress Administration project in the 1930s. Even though the one black principal in Oak Park felt that the murals should stay, the black community was divided, and the superintendent of District 97 and elected board said that they had to go. They were removed and put in storage in 1995.[131]

The second issue involved the renaming of Emerson School for poet laureate Gwendolyn Brooks at the time of the creation of the middle schools. With one of the schools already named for Percy Julian, the rationale for the choice of Emerson for a name change was that every child in Oak Park in the public school system would ultimately attend a school named after a black figure of importance. While there was little disagreement about Brooks's worth as a role model, many objected to changing the name of the one school named for the most internationally known literary figure in America while leaving other schools named after long-gone administrators intact.

At the high school, a controversy erupted in 1992 when the township drafted a policy to allow Township Youth Services to distribute condoms to teens from the age of fourteen. The school stressed abstinence, but a student who graduated in 1998 said that she and her friends handed out condoms in the bathrooms, stressing that the abstinence policy was unrealistic. Parental authority, health and religion all played a part in an ongoing discussion in this sensitive area, and the result was an agreement that no distribution would take place at the school; teens would be directed to a community wellness center for counseling and could receive condoms there.[132]

Chapter 12

ECONOMIC DEVELOPMENT AND THE
CHARACTER OF THE VILLAGE

Increasingly, in the 1990s, the overwhelming issue for Oak Park was how to increase the tax base without changing the essentially residential character of the community, an issue underscored by the upcoming 2002 centennial of the disconnection from Cicero Township and the establishment of an independent community. In addition, the fiftieth anniversary of the council/manager form of government was to be celebrated the next year, with events including a talk by the first village manager at an open board meeting. There were public events, celebrations and much to admire, but there was also fear and conflict about the best way to preserve the best of the past while moving forward to recognize new economic and social realities.

In spite of the array of new town homes and condo developments, the increasing disappearance of large families meant that homes that once held six children or more were populated by one or two adults with zero to two or three children on average. By 2000, the population had sufficiently shrunk to increase fears that the census figures would come in at under fifty thousand, causing a potential major loss of federal community development funds. Integrated, diverse and welcoming, the community now boasted three historic districts and heritage tourism, many new restaurants and schools and parks that were enjoying new facilities and support. Yet serious issues were on the table regarding the type of community Oak Park had become and was still becoming, as well as honest disagreement over to how to continue to provide the services that citizens wanted while keeping the village's already high real estate taxes from climbing higher.

Because of those issues, through the late 1990s and into the 2000s, there were many contested elections for the village, park and school boards, sometimes with several slates and occasionally with independents. The elections were exciting, with clear-cut alternatives. For the village board, both individual independents and non-VMA slates won some seats, with the board of 2005–7 being the one time that the VMA failed to hold a majority of the seats. Perhaps even more important, even though members of religious, racial and ethnic minority groups still lost many elections, others were elected, with VMA support, as members of other slates or as independents.

Although several chain restaurants and bookstores had opened on Lake Street, the last of the department stores and the branches of major retail chains had left or were leaving, most of the car dealerships were gone and the only major activity was in conversions of rental buildings into condominiums and the erection of new town homes and mid-rises. Yet the increased number of housing units, various small businesses and professional offices also put strains on public services.

At the same time, the public transportation that had been the lifeline to Chicago jobs, culture and entertainment was in danger of being compromised. The CTA proposed a package of fare increases and service cuts in 1991, including shutting the Marion Street station of what was renamed as the Green Line and the later renamed Blue Line's Lombard Station, or even closing the Austin and Oak Park Avenue stations of these lines. The president of the CTA even suggested that the Green Line could be closed completely and replaced with express buses. Soon thereafter, a downtown Chicago flood closed the Blue Line for several days, underscoring the reliance of Oak Parkers on the lines. Eventually, with the support and work of a group of Oak Park elected officials, former CTA directors and various community leaders, no changes were ever made to the stations in Oak Park other than the 1995 updating of the Marion Street Station. Over the next few years, and as part of a plan to bring together the Green Line, Metra and the Pace buses together at one location, a police substation and a couple of stores entered the mix, with a retro clock tower capping the project.

Other transportation issues were important in this era, as the village, township and various senior services tried to provide transportation for the elderly and the physically challenged. Disabled access was difficult at the newly reopened Green Line stations, and taxis were not always available, even with subsidized fares. The village sponsored a free shuttle with a fixed route, including stops in downtown Oak Park and at village hall, both for the needs of local citizens and tourists who might park and ride to the community's tourist sites. Both vans used for the shuttle service had wheelchair lifts, but the system proved wildly uneconomical, and the infrequency of rides made it impractical for seniors. After a few attempts to increase ridership, the shuttle was discontinued at the end of 2008.

The most complex set of issues relating to transportation also involved issues of ecology and the possible destruction of homes, as the Illinois Department of Transportation proposed to widen the Eisenhower Expressway. The village's response was negative, feeling that such widening would decrease the quality of life for those along the expressway, would add to air pollution, would put the conservatory and other buildings at risk and would not resolve the heaviest traffic problems along the route. In addition, a strong case was made that much more could be accomplished while serving a wider public and in a more ecologically safe way by extending the Blue Line to the western suburbs.

The idea of "capping the Ike" had first been proposed in a 1987 Illinois Department of Transportation study of air rights, and several options had been explored. However, when IDOT seriously started the process of planning the widening for high-occupancy vehicle lanes (HOV), the idea of capping at least part of the expressway received official village board support. Environmentalists and public transportation supporters such as the Citizens for Appropriate Transportation pointed out that "IDOT sees itself as a highway construction company" and that "[w]e need to force a much more careful look at alternatives."[133] Indeed, though there seemed to be several reasons to conduct a thorough environmental impact study, IDOT insisted that one was not necessary.

The village began its lobbying, in opposition to expressway widening, partially in concert with other communities along the route, and hired a law firm to represent its interests in Springfield and Washington, D.C. Simultaneously, in March 2002, the village appointed a blue-ribbon committee to keep tabs on the project and supported a "Cap the Ike" group of citizens. The economy and lack of U.S. Department of Transportation project funding put the entire project on hold, but the possibility of it being eventually funded to the exclusion of public transportation alternatives remained at the close of 2010. The lack of funding sources for a covered highway has made the proposed capping unlikely.

Largely in response to changes in the business community and the long-standing lack of parking just south of the Eisenhower, the old South Post Office was torn down at the end of the 1990s and replaced by a much larger and updated facility, with plenty of parking. The new facility was built just as far south, but now just east of Harlem Avenue. While accepting the reality

The south branch of the post office was a small building just south of the Eisenhower Expressway and had no parking. It was replaced by the new and expanded facility, on Garfield Street, east of Harlem Avenue, in 1999. *Courtesy of the author.*

that Oak Parkers wanted to maintain a high level of public services yet were frustrated by the high real estate taxes they had to bear for the rest of the twentieth century and into the twenty-first, each group of VMA village board candidates ran on a platform that included support for economic development.

The opposition parties or independent candidates tended to view the support of large development, especially with village financial involvement, as fattening the purses of developers at the expense of the taxpayers and being ruinous of the small suburban community they loved. Also, the use of TIF districts raised questions about the implications and payback for the other taxing districts affected, and that issue continued as a lively part of the political debates. Increasingly, the village response was to get involved in acquiring parcels of land that could then be sold or passed on to and help attract developers, without their having to negotiate with individual property owners to assemble large enough sites for their developments.

Even with regard to individual businesses, the village manager and the board worked, often with the OPDC, to hold on to businesses through a retail grant program and in other ways. When one of the last car dealerships, Volvo, could not survive in its Madison Street space, the village helped financially with its relocation to a visible spot on Garfield Street near the

When one of the few remaining automobile dealers on Madison Street had no place to expand its business, the village helped assure that the Volvo dealership would remain in Oak Park. The new facility is state of the art and very visible at the Harlem Blue Line exit and the ramp off the Eisenhower Expressway. *Courtesy of the author.*

Eisenhower Expressway. The village board was so committed to maintaining successful businesses that it seriously discussed a local technology company's request for support to move from its South Marion Avenue location to a vacant site on North Avenue. As all prior incentive programs had supported sales tax-generating companies, the board was loath to change direction and declined the application. Yet the issue helped broaden the discussion about both economic development and the business climate in Oak Park.[134]

Other changes relating to the business community were seen as more positive by almost everyone, especially the identification and growth of a new arts district on the several blocks of Harrison Street, between Austin Boulevard and Ridgeland Avenue. Starting with several artists/gallery owners renting inexpensive space, and then anchored by the Buzz Café at Lombard Avenue, the area grew through the 1990s, acquiring an identity, related businesses and then several restaurants. Some galleries turned into co-ops, others began to specialize in art and artifacts from other countries and still other spaces became devoted to places to learn various arts and crafts. A piece of public art was placed on the street, and street

With the increase in the number of galleries, craftsman's workshops, a framer, related businesses and restaurants, the village moved to define the blocks between Austin Boulevard and Ridgeland Avenue as the Oak Park Arts District, and the local business association sponsored and commissioned the identifying signage. *Courtesy of the author.*

exhibits came next. Music and theater became other ingredients, through performances, at festivals and on art walks, and when Val's halla, a long-established Oak Park record store, moved into the area. More recently, the business association in the area has taken on the job of serious marketing, with paid staff and active board members. Late in 2010, Open Door Repertory Company, a local theater group, was working to make a site in the area a permanent home.

The village government had a long history of commissioning studies, especially after the major planning study already discussed. During the late 1980s and through the 2000s, there were studies of the Harrison Street, the Oak Park Eisenhower area, the Chicago and Harlem Avenue area and Madison Street, as well as some broader thematic studies. In some cases, the University of Illinois at Chicago was involved, as it already had a history of working with the village, as early as designing plans and then helping with playground construction in the 1970s and up through the Harrison Corridor study, but most studies were contracted with professional consulting firms. Many of the studies involved intensive involvement by fairly small numbers of the citizenry, but critics have noted that few have resulted in real activity and change. One study that created a substantial impact came from a citizen's committee in 1999, looking at the needs of the library system. The committee concluded that the village needed both a larger and up-to-date main library and a revitalized Maze branch. The citizens approved a referendum in 2000, a home associated with Ernest Hemingway was moved and the new main library was opened in 2003.

In spite of all of the attention paid to the various retail areas throughout the village, in addition to the money that went into studies and the production of a master plan for each area, the bulk of resources, including both village and local staffing, has been concentrated on the downtown Oak Park business district. With a larger staff than any of the other groups, far more stores than in any other business district, the availability of parking garages and a tradition of hosting events like Oktoberfest, downtown Oak Park remains the heart of the business community. Yet a sensitivity to the often and loudly expressed concerns about the height of many proposed new structures, in addition to their general density, caused the split-party village board of 2005–7 to establish a development moratorium to stop the demolition of single-family homes in several areas and followed that up by the lowering of the permissible height of buildings in downtown Oak Park.[135]

After the voters of Oak Park approved a referendum, the Hemingway Interim House was relocated, and funds became available for upgrading the Maze Branch Library and building a new main library. The technologically sophisticated building opened in 2003. *Courtesy of Alan Becker.*

In the post-mall era, downtown Oak Park is not only a shopping area but also a marketing entity, with its own sales, promotions and events. This recent flyer indicates the range and variety of the advertising and includes webpage information. *Courtesy of Downtown Oak Park.*

Adding that initiative to the reality of the three historic districts in the community, fewer teardowns of residential properties occurred in the boom years of the early 2000s than in communities like Hinsdale and Elmhurst. Though there have not been many teardowns, the size of additions to existing homes has raised concerns about creeping gigantic development and the impact on the neighbors of those who have made drastic changes to their homes with additions that sometimes have equaled the square footage of the whole original house. However, the lack of more affordable housing has been a much larger issue in the twenty-first century.

The condo conversion craze that made conversion from apartments financially attractive to the owners of apartment buildings has made the condo apartment the "starter house" for many families. As early as 2000, the village board studied the condo conversion issue, with the township assessor pointing out that there was no guarantee of a substantial increase in the tax base due to conversions because of the lower tax assessment rate on homes than rental units. What was worrying segments of the community and the board was more than the "dwindling number of apartments available for rent in Oak Park, but the possibility that trend is eroding the economic diversity of the Village."[136] Within a few years that issue was magnified, and the addition of almost all new housing in the form of condos, town homes or high-end rental units caused concerned citizens to push the Plan Commission to add affordable housing to the list of possible compensating benefits a developer might offer to win approval of a planned development. Other suggestions were for allowing basement bedrooms in apartment houses, creating more three-bedroom apartments by combining units to accommodate more families and taking other initiatives. At the same time, the Residence Corporation was keeping a vigilant eye on deteriorating rental buildings, managing them when possible and working with the Code Department of the village and the Housing Center to maintain the quality of the diminished number of rental units. However, much of the attention that had been paid to housing in regard to diversity and resegregation, through the staff of the Community Relations Division and village programs, was starting to fade. The number of staff in Community Relations diminished through the 2000s, and the counseling program disappeared. These changes were seen as dangerous mistakes by some and proof that such programs were no longer needed by others.

Housing and development issues have generated the most passion for decades, but other changes to historic practices and customs have also been the subject of major debate. It was already noted that the appropriate attire for graduations at the high school has been reviewed and voted on many times, but that tradition long in effect persists, now with the women allowed to wear white pantsuits instead of dresses. The biggest controversy, one that took several years to resolve and was the subject of lengthy hearings by the zoning board and then the Plan Commission, was the move to install lights at a high school athletic field to permit late afternoon practice and evening games. Much passion was in evidence, with the neighbors taking the usual position that the change boded ill for their quality of life and was unnecessary. At the same time, the high school and athletic boosters spoke in favor of change and new needs. Eventually, the village board approved a somewhat scaled-down proposal, and the first nighttime game was held in September 2009.

However, a more serious battle concerns "the achievement gap," a disparity of scores on standardized tests, on college admissions and grades, between white and minority students. The District 200 and, to a somewhat lesser extent, District 97 Boards have been working hard to understand both the why and the how of the problem, but with far less than the hoped-for success to date. Something is happening after the students start school and before they reach the high school, in spite of the reorganization into the middle school concept. The issue is somewhat polarizing, with many black families citing institutionalized discrimination and lower expectation for black students and many whites claiming that the students are treated the same way but are not acting the same way. While this is seen primarily as an issue of race, an African American teacher and board member of District 200 has raised other issues concerning the gap, suggesting that the solution involves raising the level for all students. The discussion will be a defining one for the immediate future.[137]

The Westgate area was a major focus point for years, both on its own part, with a lot of turnover in the small storefronts, and in conjunction with the possible redevelopment of the Colt Building and the possible creation of new traffic patterns and parking spaces. Ironically, this set of storefront buildings, which had been the site of destruction of the homes of African Americans in 1929, was now part of the focus of preservation efforts. The Colt Building itself, erected in 1931, was Art Deco style on the Lake Street side and Tudor style facing Westgate. The village sought site proposals that could either incorporate the building or not. When nobody came forth with appropriate proposals, another round of demolition took place, in advance of any new development.

At the same time, the remaining part of the 1970s mall, South Marion Street, was opened to traffic in 2007 to great fanfare. Again there was hope that the right combination of parking, street landscaping and amenities would help produce a healthy retail environment. The lot, still empty at this writing, on Lake Street was made into temporary parking, and a new midweek market of local vendors opened in the summer of 2010.

The Shops of Downtown Oak Park was one the first of the major developments, with several long-established businesses on the site either

Above: After it was clear that there were no immediate development possibilities for the Colt Building, demolition took place from Westgate to Lake Streets, and a parking lot replaced the buildings. In the summer of 2010, an outdoor market occupied the site on Wednesdays. *Courtesy of the Village of Oak Park.*

Below: The reopening of Marion Street signaled the end of an era. Crowds of residents explored the stores, examined the streetscape and enjoyed refreshments in spite of the cold weather; then they joined their neighbors in this group photo on November 21, 2007. *Courtesy of the Village of Oak Park.*

moving to make way for the development or reconfigured in the new space. After several false starts in the area in the mid-1990s, the wrecking ball went to work. Already, as that development took form, other project proposals appeared at the Planning Department of the village—mostly, but not exclusively, for the downtown area. The mixed-use projects at Ridgeland Avenue and South Boulevard and others—including the Opera House, the RSC Building, the Whiteco project and the never-developed Colt space— were the most controversial, with all but one meant to contain a combination of housing and retail.

In March 2010, the village board gave its unanimous approval to the proposal for a nineteen-story combination hotel, condo, retail and parking project at Lake and Forest, with the village committing some $10 million toward the garage and more for the guarantee on the hotel.[138] Though the project remains on hold due to a soft economy and the inability of the developer to gain financing, it is the latest in the series of projects bitterly opposed by residents in the area (and others) who object to the height, insufficient parking,

Community Bank of Oak Park River Forest was opened in 1996 on the site of the former Great American Savings Bank, on the corner of Lake Street and Forest Avenue. With a branch west on Lake Street in River Forest, it remains the only locally owned and operated banking facility. *Courtesy of Community Bank of Oak Park River Forest.*

traffic concerns and the scale in relationship to the neighboring historic district, all complicated this time by the hotel portion. Village boards have sought a new hotel for decades. Opponents, however, have cited insufficient demand, given Oak Park as a side trip for people visiting Chicago or staying at airport area hotels. Opponents also see a probably negative impact on the two hotels already located in the community, but the elected trustees have consistently supported proposals to bring a hotel to the community.

One of the strengths of Oak Park had always been its locally owned and operated banking and savings institutions, all the way to before the creation of an independent village. As noted, the major banking institutions all survived the Depression of the 1930s, yet most disappeared as independent entities in the consolidations of the 1980s and 1990s and in bank collapses of the 2000s. In 2009, Park National (long First Oak Park) Bank was taken over, leaving Community Bank of Oak Park River Forest as the only banking facility in the community still owned by local investors. Opened in 1996, Community Bank, too, has had its outstanding loan portfolio rigorously examined and had to raise funds in 2010 to avoid regulatory action. Luckily, the bank was able to do so and survives as an institution in and for the community in which it is based.

The issue of gun control seemed to be resolved a score of years earlier, but the case that eventually reached the U.S. Supreme Court brought an unusually high degree of cooperation between Oak Park and Chicago. Rather than reversing its gun bans in the same way as several other suburbs did, the president of the village and the mayor of Chicago worked together, as Oak Park joined Chicago with an amicus brief. When the justices ruled against Chicago, pro-gun advocates were elated. But Oak Park was quick to begin work on trying to make the most stringent rules for gun ownership that could be defended in court and still show its penchant for reform.

A decade into the twenty-first century, the Village of Oak Park finds itself with challenges and the pull of varying forces. Committed to making Oak Park a "green" community, the village board had authorized the rebuilding of a public works center after a major fire. The center was opened in 2007 and recognized as a Gold LEED Certified building. Bicycling in the community has been encouraged, with additional bike racks being included as a compensating benefit in many of the newer developments, with energy efficiency being supported wherever possible. Yet the push for development—and the invariable developer response of engaging in new construction over rehabilitation and adaptive reuse—belies the fact that the "greenest" building is the one that is already there.

Pictured is the open house at the dedication of the new Gold LEED Certified public works building in late 2007; this was Illinois' first public works facility to obtain LEED certification. All of the supplies, repair facilities and other functions are under one green roof. *Courtesy of the Village of Oak Park.*

The need to respect both the appearance of the historic architecture itself and the impact it has on those who live in it was underscored in 2010 when the American Planning Association listed the Frank Lloyd Wright Historic District area as one of the ten best neighborhoods in which to live in the United States. Coming on the heels of a 2009 rating of Oak Park as one of the ten best places for affluent singles in the country (and with a third of the population so classified), it is clear that Oak Park is no longer the quiet village of large single-family homes filled with large families that it was at its founding and for years thereafter.[139] However, at the same time, there is concern that the village is unaffordable for lower-income individuals and even the children of long-established families.

The population of the village has been in decline for decades from a postwar high of 62,511 in 1970. Despite the construction of new town homes and condo buildings, smaller families, couples without children and the increasing number of singles fail to offset the loss. The attraction of people of diverse backgrounds and heritages continues, with the 2010 census figures substantiating the trend. Overall, the population decreased by a little more than 1.0 percent since the 2000 census, but the diversity figures are more interesting. The white population dropped by 2.8 percent, while the black population dropped by 4.7 percent. The number of Hispanic and Asian residents, though still small, grew by 48.3 percent and about 50.0 percent, respectively.[140] Though the issues of affordability and access are still of lesser or greater concern to individuals, officials and organizations, the efforts of those who fought for open housing and racial integration without resegregation seem to have been remarkably successful.

The population of the village has also become increasingly liberal politically. In 1967, a scholar noted that Oak Park "has never voted for a Democratic candidate for the American presidency," yet the percent of votes for President Obama exceeded 84 percent in 2008.[141] But that is not to say that there are not still many on both sides of the political divide, with others in between and further out of the mainstream parties. Such differences continue to make for passionate dialogue and often strong disagreement.

The tensions that arose with the efforts of the first "reformers" to abolish the sale of liquor and the reaction of those who disagreed are still part of the dynamic of the community. The exclusion of national political parties from local elections is still seen as an unqualified good by the supporters of slating caucuses, and others still decry elitism. The attempt to provide housing for people of diverse economic backgrounds often comes into conflict in regard to class and lifestyle issues. Respecting the character and traditions of the past while becoming an ever more diverse community, open to ideas from all segments of the population, and blending income-producing economic development with sustainable and environmentally friendly homes and businesses is the challenge for the future.

NOTES

CHAPTER 1

1. William Dring, *The Continental Divide in Oak Park*, website, revised 2007. Dring, the force behind the recognition and signage for the divide in Oak Park, relied on the scientific writing of H. Harlen Bretz and his *Geology of the Chicago Region*, a report for the Illinois Geological Survey of 1939 (oprf. com/divide).

2. Ulrich Danckers and Jane Meredith, *A Compendium of the Early History of Chicago to the Year 1835 When the Indians Left* (River Forest, IL: Early Chicago, Inc., 2000), 16–17. The first of the marriages mentioned is of one of La Salle's men marrying an Indian woman at Chicagou in 1692.

3. The map was drawn by Guillaune Delisle.

4. Danckers and Meredith, *Compendium of the Early History*, 20.

5. Alfred T. Andreas, *History of Cook County* (Chicago, IL: Western Historical Society, 1884), 116.

CHAPTER 2

6. When the Community Bank of Oak Park and River Forest was opened in the mid-1990s, they paid homage to the early name by offering an "Oak Ridge Account."

7. Jean Guarino, *Yesterday: A Historical View of Oak Park, Illinois*, vol. 1, *Prairie Days to World War I* (Oak Park, IL: Oak Ridge Press, 2000), 5. Guarino cites Kettlestrings's son, Walter, as the source for the information about the additional land purchase.

8. Weston A. Goodspeed and Daniel D. Healy, eds., *History of Cook County, Illinois* (Chicago, IL: Goodspeed Historical Association, 1909), 294.

9. James B. Herrick, *Memories of Eighty Years*, revised ed. (Chicago, IL: University of Chicago Press, 1949), 2.

10. Harvey M. Karlen, "Whatever Happened to Noyesville," *Illinois Postal Historian* 16, no. 2 (May 1995): 6.

11. Goodspeed and Healy, *History of Cook County, Illinois*, 292.

12. Gertrude Fox Hoagland, ed., "Historical Survey of Oak Park, Illinois," unpublished Federal Works Progress Administration Project manuscript, 1937, 101–3. Collection of the Oak Park Public Library and the Historical Society of Oak Park and River Forest.

13. Edwin O. Gale, *Reminiscences of Early Chicago and Vicinity* (Chicago, IL: Fleming H. Revell Co., 1902), 421.

14. William E. Barton, *Glimpses of Oak Park* (Oak Park, IL: Frank H. June and George R. Hemingway, Publishers, 1912), unpaged.

Chapter 3

15. Herrick, *Memories of Eighty Years*, 17.

16. Gale, *Reminiscences of Early Chicago*, 416–17.

17. Ibid., 420.

18. Ibid., 421.

19. Guarino, *Yesterday*, 49.

20. The law called for heavy license fees and insurance and gave the opportunity for almost anyone to sue the bar owner for damages as a result of accidents, injury or death after being served liquor.

21. Barton, *Glimpses of Oak Park*.

22. Hoagland, "Historical Survey of Oak Park, Illinois," 53.

23. "History of the Main Library." Oak Park Public Library website, oppl. org/main/history.htm.

24. Hoagland, "Historical Survey of Oak Park, Illinois," 127.

25. *Oak Park Argus*, 1902. Collection of the Historical Society of Oak Park and River Forest.

26. Horace B. Humphrey, *Oak Leaves*, March 18, 1916, carried a story about the issue.

27. Hoagland, "Historical Survey of Oak Park, Illinois," 63.

28. Ibid., 59.

29. Gale, *Reminiscences of Early Chicago*, 422–23.

30. John Stanger, "The Oak Parker Who Assassinated a President," June 29, 2010, www.wednesdayjournalonline.com.

31. *Vindicator*, March 8, 1884.

32. Hoagland, "Historical Survey of Oak Park, Illinois," 51.

33. May Estelle Cook, *Little Old Oak Park: 1837–1902* (Oak Park, IL: privately printed, 1961), 36.

34. Herrick, *Memories of Eighty Years*, 3.

35. Jeanette Fields, "Apartment Building Architects Prove Nay Sayers Wrong," *Wednesday Journal*, April 4, 1984, 11. Fields also discussed the way two flats were disguised as single-family homes.

36. Stan West, Peggy Tuck Sinko and Frank Lipo, with Yves Hughes Jr., *Suburban Promised Land: The Emerging Black Community in Oak Park, Illinois, 1880–1980* (Oak Park, IL: Soweto Press and the Historical Society of Oak Park and River Forest, 2009), 8.

37. Hoagland, "Historical Survey of Oak Park, Illinois," 117.

38. Ibid., 109.

Chapter 4

39. Hoagland, "Historical Survey of Oak Park, Illinois," 22

40. Clearly, the other communities wanted out of a township in which they felt that their interests were not represented.

41. John Lewis, *President's Report to the Township of Cicero*, April 14, 1900, Township of Cicero Reports, 1896–1901. Collection of Historical Society of Oak Park and River Forest.

Chapter 5

42. Erwin E. Bach., *A Short History of Oak Park Township, 1903–1987* (Oak Park, IL: privately printed, 1987), 1.

43. Oak Park Board of Trustees, *First Annual Report: January 1st, 1902–December 31st, 1902* (Oak Park, IL: Ainsworth and Wilson, 1903), 4–5.

44. *Oak Leaves*, "Oak Park vs. Cicero," April 11, 1902, 10.

45. *Oak Leaves*, "A Township Merger," April 10, 1903, 12.

46. Hoagland, "Historical Survey of Oak Park, Illinois," 96.

47. Village of Oak Park, *Annual Report for 1908*, 5. Collection of the Historical Society of Oak Park and River Forest.

48. "History of the Main Library," Oak Park Public Library website.

Chapter 6

49. Barton, *Glimpses of Oak Park*, first page.

50. *Oak Leaves*, October 8, 1910.

51. *Oak Park Reporter Argus*, "Three Hundred New Houses Will Make Village of Prairie Land," May 19, 1906.

52. Lee Brooke, *Yesterday When I Was Younger* (Oak Park, IL: privately printed, 1989), 122.

53. Guarino, *Yesterday*, 72.

54. Ascension Parish of Oak Park, *Ascension Centennial Book, 1907–2007* (Oak Park, IL: Ascension Parish, 2007).

55. West, Sinko and Lipo, *Suburban Promised Land*, 17. The authors quote an *Oak Leaves* article of August 22, 1902.

56. Ibid., 27.

57. Rush Oak Park Hospital, unpublished historical timeline of the hospital that was drafted for its 2007 centennial celebration, internal document, courtesy of the marketing and communications coordinator.

58. W.R. Kendall, "Street Names Again," *Oak Leaves*, April 25, 1902, 8.

59. Ibid.

60. *Oak Leaves*, January 18, 1913.

61. Hoagland, "Historical Survey of Oak Park, Illinois," 60.

62. Village of Oak Park, *Annual Reports of the Village of Oak Park, Cook County, Illinois, January 1, 1911 to December 31, 1911, Published by the Order of the Board of Trustees*, 63–65. Collection of the Historical Society of Oak Park and River Forest.

63. Guarino, *Yesterday*, 110.

64. *Oak Leaves*, January 15, 1916, 1.

65. Park District of Oak Park, *Minutes of the Park District of Oak Park*, Oak Park, Illinois.

66. *Annual Play Festival Brochure*, Holmes School, Oak Park, June 6, 1914.

CHAPTER 7

67. *Chicago Daily Tribune*, "Oak Park States Warmest Fight of Small Towns," April 2, 1919, 9.

68. *Oak Leaves*, October 1, 1921, 1.

69. West, Sinko and Lipo, *Suburban Promised Land*, 30.

70. *Oak Leaves*, May 19, 1928, 144.

71. Hoagland, "Historical Survey of Oak Park, Illinois," 82–83.

72. Though there were lingering concerns about Lake Michigan's water, there was no longer a fear of a water shortage.

73. *Oak Leaves*, December 24, 1927, 32.

74. Thanks to Faith Humphrey-Hill, executive director of the Oak Park Art League, for her help and information.

75. Oak Park Public Library website.

76. Hoagland, "Historical Survey of Oak Park, Illinois," 171.

77. Oak Park–River Forest High School website, www.oprfhs.org/about_us/History.html.

78. John H. Stoddard, ed., "The Review: Reunion 50 Oak Park Junior College," unpublished pamphlet, December 1988. Collection of the Historical Society of Oak Park and River Forest.

79. Oak Park Historic Preservation Commission, *Ridgeland Revealed: Guide to the Architecture of the Ridgeland–Oak Park Historic District*. (Oak Park, IL: Village of Oak Park, 1993), 9.

80. *Oak Leaves*, "Editorial," August 23, 1913, 16.

81. *Oak Leaves*, "Court Supports Zoning," August 23, 1921.

82. Bevanee Marshal Matlack, "Discusses Zoning," *Oak Leaves*, July 30, 1927, 54–55.

83. *Oak Leaves*, "Ordinance to Regulate Rooming Houses Voted," March 7, 1940, 1.

84. *Oak Leaves*, November 5, 1921, 99.

85. West, Sinko and Lipo, *Suburban Promised Land*, 43.

86. *Oak Parker*, March 24, 1933.

87. *Oak Leaves*, "Appeal to State Chief," February 1, 1930. 1, 24.

88. Ibid.

Chapter 8

89. *Oak Leaves*, "Trustees Act To Halt Rent Gouging," July 18, 1946, 1.

90. *Oak Leaves*, "Park Land Voted for Vet Houses," August 25, 1946.

91. *Oak Leaves*, "111 Families Face Loss of Housing Here," April 7, 1949, 1.

92. *Oak Leaves*, "Question of Highway Ramps Brings Petitions," October 11, 1955, 5.

93. Sarah L. Guerin, "The History of the Eisenhower Expressway in Oak Park," unpublished paper at Historical Society of Oak Park and River Forest, unpaged. From an interview with Peggy Studney.

94. Park District of Oak Park minutes, housed at the Park District offices in Oak Park.

95. *Oak Leaves*, "New Trustees Sworn In," April 16, 1921, 1.

96. Ken Trainor, "How a Great Books Group Led to a Political Revolution," *Wednesday Journal*, Special Section, November, 2001, 14.

97. Nathan Helsabeck, "The VMA: The Struggle for Political Independence in Suburban Chicago," unpublished paper, University of Illinois at Chicago, December, 13, 2006.

98. *Oak Leaves*, March 23, 1950.

99. This anecdote was so symbolic of the change from the old guard to the new way of doing things that it was quoted in the local papers, histories and even in the *Chicago Tribune* at a later date.

100. West Suburban Congregation Har Zion, "History," wsthz.org/pages/history.html.

101. Village of Oak Park, "Proclamation of Barber Shop Day in Oak Park," Village Board Minutes, June 22, 1955.

102. Park Board of Oak Park minutes, August 11, 1969.

103. *Oak Leaves*, March 16, 1950.

104. Robert Wesley Giles, "Government, Race and Elementary Education in Oak Park, Illinois: A Case History of Decision Making," PhD dissertation, University of Illinois at Urbana, 1988.

105. West, Sinko and Lipo, *Suburban Promised Land*, 66.

106. Ibid., 86.

CHAPTER 9

107. Village of Oak Park minutes, December 19, 1966.

108. Ibid., June 17, 1968.

109. Ibid., November 6, 1967.

110. Ibid., May 18, 1970.

111. Carole Goodwin, *The Oak Park Strategy* (Chicago, IL: University of Chicago Press, 1979), 126.

112. Roberta L. Raymond, "The Challenge to Oak Park: A Suburban Community Faces Racial Change," MA thesis, Roosevelt University, 1972, 88.

113. Goodwin, *Oak Park Strategy*, 188. The chapter on "Voluntary Organizations" contains detailed information on several other organizations and their structure as well.

114. E-mail communication from Galen Gockel, December 30, 2010.

115. *Chicago Tribune, NE*, "Bid to Abolish Township in Oak Park Defeated," April 17, 1970, 6.

116. Village of Oak Park minutes, November 17, 1969.

117. Mary L. Piccoli, "The Effect of Major Shopping Centers on the Retail Sales of Oak Park, Illinois," unpublished paper, Rosary College, March 31, 1971, 23.

118. *Economist*, April 24–25, 1973, 1.

CHAPTER 10

119. Park District of Oak Park website, oakparkparks.com/AboutUs/history.htm.

120. Frederick C. Klein, "How Oak Park Staved Off Blight," *Wall Street Journal*, November 11, 1976.

121. Dan Haley, "Editorial," *Wednesday Journal*, September 4, 1985, 12.

CHAPTER 11

122. Bob Miodonski, "Protestors Drown Out Nazi Rhetoric," *Oak Leaves*, October 1, 1980, 5.

123. The local press covered the issue extensively, people on both sides of the issue met in homes and both sides submitted petitions to the District 200 Board.

124. The author was serving on the village board from 1977 through 1981, and at least one caller identified himself and asked me if I wanted my wife raped by n******. He warned that it could happen if they knew we didn't have guns.

125. Laslo Tako, "Viewpoints," *Wednesday Journal*, December 16, 1992.

126. *Oak Leaves*, "Anatomy of a Project: Stankus Hole to 100 Forest," February 7, 1999.

127. Bryan Miller, "Offices the Trend on the Mall," *Wednesday Journal*, March 20, 1985, 27.

128. *Chicago Tribune*, September 6, 1987, Section 7, 3.

129. Susan Montgomery, "CAST Celebrates 10th Anniversary," *Oak Leaves*, April 26, 1995, 16.

130. Lisa Brown, "New Middle Schools on Time, Under Budget," *Wednesday Journal*, July 10, 2002.

131. Mary L. Gray, *A Guide to Chicago's Murals* (Chicago, IL: University of Chicago Press, 2001), 380.

132. Chris LaFortune, "OPRF to Compromise on Condom Use," *Oak Leaves*, June 25, 2003.

CHAPTER 12

133. Cheri Bentrup, "CATS Brings Residents Up to Date on Eisenhower," *Oak Leaves*, March 13, 2002, 13.

134. *Wednesday Journal*, "After Decades of Grants to Retailers, OP Eyes Pros, Cons of Service Subsidies," September 28, 2005.

135. *Wednesday Journal*, January 29, 2007.

136. Cheri Bentrup, "Condo Conversion Impact Studied," *Oak Leaves*, March 15, 2000, 7.

137. Ralph Lee, "Taking Another Look at the Achievement Gap at OPRF," *Wednesday Journal*, November 30, 2010.

138. Village of Oak Park minutes, March 18, 2010.

139. The CNN website cnnmoney.com produced the survey and rating, with Oak Park listed in seventh place.

140. Todd Shields, "Oak Park's Population Drops Slightly," *Oak Leaves*, February 24, 2011, 3.

141. Arthur Evans Le Gacy, "Improvers and Preservers: A History of Oak Park, Illinois, 1833–1940," PhD dissertation, University of Chicago, 1967, 1.

INDEX

ABOUT THE AUTHOR

David M. Sokol is professor emeritus and former chair of the Department of Art History at University of Illinois at Chicago, where he taught American art and directed the program in museology. He began teaching at UIC in 1971 and still directs the work of several graduate students. He also served as a museum curator and administrator and is the author of many exhibition catalogues for museums, college galleries, art centers and commercial galleries.

He served a term as a trustee on the Oak Park Village Board from 1977 to 1981, several years on the Plan Commission and many years as chair of the Historic Preservation Commission. Sokol served as vice-president of the Unity Temple Restoration Foundation and as a member of the board of the Frank Lloyd Wright Home and Studio Foundation. He currently chairs the Oak Park Public Art Advisory Commission and recently completed a term on the Illinois Historic Sites Advisory Council. He was elected to the Oak Park Library Board in April 2011. Sokol is also a past president of the American Culture Association.

In addition to his other books, articles, reviews and exhibition catalogues on both American and European art and architecture, Sokol is the author of *Oak Park, Illinois: Continuity and Change* and co-author of the guidebook to the Prairie School District of Oak Park and has written a monograph on Frank Lloyd Wright's Unity Temple, *The Noble Room*.

ALSO BY DAVID M. SOKOL

John Quidor: Painter of American Legend (1973)

American Architecture and Art: A Guide to Information Sources (1976)

American Art: Painting, Sculpture, Architecture, Decorative Arts, Photography (co-author, 1979)

American Decorative Arts and Old World Influences: A Guide to Information Sources (1980)

Life in Nineteenth-Century America (1981)

Solitude: Inner Visions in American Art (1982)

Two Hundred Years of American Painting from Chicago Private Collections (1983)

American Art: American Vision, Paintings from a Century of Collecting, co-author (1990)

A Guide to Oak Park's Frank Lloyd Wright and the Prairie School Historic District (co-author, 1999)

Oak Park, Illinois: Continuity and Change (2000)

Engaging with the Present: The Contribution of the American Jewish Artists Club to Modern Art in Chicago (2004)

Otto Neumann: His Life and Work (2007)

The Noble Room (2008)

Curt Frankenstein: Dream World and Real World (2009)